The very existence of the Christian community is under attack.

The Jonestown tragedy is perhaps Satan's most significant attack on Christianity in the twentieth century. What happened there and why? In this very different book about the People's Temple in San Francisco, Mel White approaches the subject from an evangelical perspective—seeing the evil clearly and asking how Christians could have prevented this terrible event. Based on personal interviews with defectors from the People's Temple, survivors of the Jonestown massacre, and parents and friends of those who died in the jungles of Guyana, the author demonstrates how the Reverend Jim Jones had deceived most of the world. He gives meaning to the tragic deaths, asking "What can we do to keep it from happening again?"

By Mel White

In the Presence of Mine Enemies (with Lyla White, Howard and Phyllis Rutledge)
Tested by Fire (with Merrill and Virginia Womach and Lyla White)
Lust: The Other Side of Love
Deceived

DECEIVED

Mel White

*With Paul Scotchmer
and Marguerite Shuster*

SPIRE BOOKS

Fleming H. Revell Company
Old Tappan, New Jersey

ISBN 0-8007-8367-0
Library of Congress Catalog Card Number: 79-1519
A Spire Book
Copyright© 1979 by Mel White
Published by Fleming H. Revell Company
All rights reserved
Printed in the United States of America

This is an original Spire book, published by Spire Books, a Division
of Fleming H. Revell Company, Old Tappan, New Jersey.

"I hope that your kids can be saved by our kids being slaughtered."

MRS. CLARE BOUQUET
Mother of Bryan, killed at Jonestown

Contents

Introduction:
The House on
Regent Street

This book is *not* about Jonestown. Pictures of that tragic jungle massacre are already printed indelibly on our minds. This *is* a book about people who died there, about others who escaped, and about Jim Jones who deceived them. It is my attempt to answer the questions each of us has asked, "How could it happen?"—and "What can we do to keep it from happening again?" While the body count went on in Guyana and military teams worked to identify the victims of the massacre, I flew to San Francisco, rented a car, and drove across the bay to Berkeley. Though reporters from the world's press were rummaging through the ruins of Jonestown, I believed that the answers to our questions about this tragedy lay with a handful of people gathered in a yellow, wood-frame house on Regent Street.

After Congressman Leo Ryan's murder, police and federal marshals surrounded this same old house with barricades while SWAT teams patrolled the neighborhood with high-powered rifles and binoculars. Over the next few days most of the people who gathered at 3028 Regent Street were either defectors from the People's Temple who had organized this Human Freedom Center as a place of refuge for cult defectors; or members of Concerned Relatives, families of Jonestown settlers who had been working to insure the freedom and well-being of their loved ones in Jonestown. Members of Concerned Relatives had accompanied Ryan to Guyana and were returning in shock and disbelief. Because both groups were high on Jones's retaliatory "hit list," they were being guarded by police agencies for their own protection.

Some gathered in the long living room on secondhand couches or lay back on the worn green rug watching a vintage black and white television screen. Others sat around the large dining-room table, drinking coffee and thumbing slowly through the growing mound of print and pictures on Jonestown gathered from newspapers and magazines. They comforted each other when family or friends were recognized in pictures of the tangled bodies. They encouraged each other with happy memories. They came and went, drawn together by their common hope and their common horror. Television crews, reporters, FBI agents, and police were in and out, adding to the noisy confusion of the scene.

In the midst of all of this I came, a Christian

writer and filmmaker, interested in finding answers to the questions Jonestown raises for the church. When I knocked on the door, a voice behind a curtained glass asked, "How can we help you?" After I identified myself, Jean Mills, a People's Temple defector who, with her husband, Al, founded the Center, listened patiently to my explanation and seemed quite enthusiastic about getting their story "to the place where it might help the most." Jean introduced me to their volunteer spokesperson, Holli Morton, who arranged the lengthy interviews from which my observations are drawn.

For four weeks I was in San Francisco, trying to find answers from defectors from the People's Temple, survivors of the Jonestown massacre, and parents and friends of those who died. As the rumors of a hit list grew, and my subjects were placed under police protection or went into temporary hiding—as the full extent of the ugliness and horror of the People's Temple became known to me—and as the full-color pictures of bloating bodies and first-person accounts of the horror were exploited endlessly—I had the growing urge to run from that awful jungle carnage and to refuse to think about it again.

But I mustn't forget it; I can't let the jungle grow back over Jonestown. It is too easy to blame the madman Jones, his henchmen and women, and walk away. It is too simplistic to give Satan all the credit and just use Jonestown as one more awful example of the powers of darkness at work in this world. And though it is true that there was very little that was Christian about the People's Temple Christian Church, it is not true that Jonestown has nothing to teach us who see ourselves as "real Christians."

Besides, those who died deserve better from us. By our asking honestly, "How could it happen?" and "What can we do to keep it from happening again?" we give some meaning to their tragic deaths. They were our neighbors, and they were deceived. According to NBC, there are eight million other Americans already deceived by the cults, and every day the number grows. If I have learned anything from Jonestown, it is that those events could happen again. By looking closely at this tragic moment in Christian history, we may learn our lessons in time.

For Reflection and Discussion

Following each chapter of this book is a series of questions for readers to reflect upon and discuss. The questions are aimed at encouraging Christians to look honestly in three directions: at the Scriptures, at themselves, and at their own churches and fellowship groups. And even before we have formally begun to face the story of Jonestown, as set down in these pages, there are some preliminary questions worth considering. Reflect on those that follow and write down your thoughts, *before* you read further.

1. Do you consider yourself vulnerable in any way to "conversion" by a cult? How? or why not?
2. How might other members of your church or fellowship group be vulnerable?
3. Read Colossians 2:8 and keep it in mind as you continue to read. Jones's philosophy was pragmatism: he often repeated that "the end justifies the means." Do you agree? Always? Ever? *Deceit* was his key tool. When, if ever, do you think deceit is justifiable?

Scripture Text

Colossians 2:8
See to it that no one makes a prey of you by philosophy and empty deceit, according to human tradition, according to the elemental spirits of the universe, and not according to Christ.

1

Jones's Victims Were From Our Churches

What led them to the Temple?

It will take years to unravel the mystery of Jonestown. There are no statistics gathered about the people who were brainwashed and deceived by "the Reverend Jim Jones." There are no records available to us giving names, addresses, and personality profiles of those who came to People's Temple Christian Church and stayed to die. The puzzle must be assembled piece by piece from the handful of surviving defectors and relatives of the dead.

I asked each of my subjects to describe his religious background, hoping to prove that the converts to Jones's false version of the Christian faith might not have been deceived—*if* they had been exposed to some version of true Christian faith when they were children. After all, we Christians spend a lot of time and money on the Christian education of our children. Seldom do we have a chance like this one to see if it makes a difference.

They Were Exposed to Christian Truth as Children

It was in a long interview with Tim Stoen in a back room of the house on Regent Street that I got my first answer to that question. Tim was once the second most powerful man in People's Temple. Tim has a law degree from Stanford University and served as an Assistant District Attorney for San Francisco, until he resigned to go to Jonestown in 1977. Tim defected from the cult last year and worked tirelessly, until that awful Saturday in November, to get his son John Victor, age six, away from Jones and the jungle. According to eyewitness accounts, little "John-John" was found dead beside Jones's body.

Could a strong Christian background have made the difference? If Tim Stoen had been exposed to Christian education from his childhood, could this tragedy have been averted in his life and in the life of his family? Tim answered my question without hesitating:

"I was raised in a Christian home," he told me. "My parents were fundamentalists, members of the General Association of Regular Baptists [GARB]. I went to Sunday school and church all my young life. I attended Wheaton College [a leading evangelical Christian college in Illinois] and was involved in student leadership. When I moved to California, I joined and attended regularly the First Presbyterian Church in Berkeley. For two years I was the president of their Corinthians, a business and professional young-adult group. I admired and respected their evangelical yet socially concerned pastoral staff. I was attending First Presbyterian and the People's Temple, until I joined Jim Jones's staff in Ukiah."

Jean Mills, for seven years a member of the Temple, one of Jones's writers and a member of the Planning Commission, attended a Seventh Day Adventist Sabbath school. "I attended or taught in my church's Christian education program from my childhood," she told me. "When I was eighteen years old, I was the leader of the Pathfinders Club, which had over fifty kids in it; and I had twenty-two adults working under me. I could give you an answer from the Bible for any question. I knew the Bible backward and forward. At one point in my life, the minister tried to send me to college to become his Bible worker. I was very dedicated to the church."

Catholic education didn't fare any better than its Protestant counterpart. Grace Stoen grew up in a Catholic home, attended parochial schools, and went to weekly cathechism for ten years in San Francisco; yet for five years Grace headed the Temple's 120 counselors and at the Wednesday-night family meetings passed on to Jones the names of Temple members to be disciplined that week.

Bryan Bouquet, who died in Jonestown, allegedly told Congressman Ryan before his death, "The next time I see my mother, I want it to be down the barrel of a rifle." Yet Bryan Bouquet, before being brainwashed by Jones, attended Catholic schools through the eighth grade. Al Mills, another member of the Temple's Planning Commission, grew up in Catholic schools, lived in a convent school for a year and a half when he was a child, and in adult life served as chairman for a Council of Churches commission.

I found religious background in everyone I interviewed. Wayne Pietila was a member of the People's Temple for seven years. He had served on the powerful Planning Commission of the cult and had acted as Jones's private bodyguard and driver. Yet Wayne grew up in Nazarene Sunday schools. Lena, his wife and longtime member of the cult, grew up in a charismatic church and attended Sunday school and church regularly. Bonnie Thielmann, for six years a member of the Temple, was the daughter of Assembly of God missionaries to Brazil and attended Bethany College, a Lutheran school in Minnesota. Carolyn Moore was president of her Methodist Youth Fellowship group. She and her sister, Annie, were both children of a Methodist minister; yet the Moore sisters served as intimate Jones aides, and both died in Guyana. Maria Katsaris, another of Jones's aides and mistresses, was the daughter of a former Greek Orthodox priest.

Once it had been established that all my subjects had at least some exposure to Christian truth when they were children, and many of them had taken responsible adult roles in Catholic and Protestant churches as well, the obvious next question was "What went wrong?" Why did these people give up the Christianity of their childhood for Jones and the People's Temple?

As I talked to these Temple defectors, it became apparent that their dissatisfaction with their Christian past revolved around two major themes. First, the Christian people in their experience didn't seem to love each other inside the church. And second, Christian people didn't seem to love the needy outside the church.

They Didn't Feel Love in Our Churches

Jeannie Mills expressed what I heard in different ways from so many ex-Temple members. Her disillusionment began at a time of crisis in her life when her church—out of firmly held convictions—failed to give her the support she needed. It continued as she vainly sought warmth and acceptance in other churches. But here is her story:

For fifteen years Jeannie worked hard in her church as a teacher and in other volunteer capacities. She had struggled in the early years of her marriage to help put her husband through Bible school, so that he might become a minister in their denomination. When she was twenty-nine her marriage failed. Jeannie and her first husband were divorced. Eventually she expressed her desire to remarry—and so began her journey to the People's Temple.

"The church fathers called me and suggested that they understood how these things go, but by the rules of the church the first person to remarry was committing adultery; and that I could save everybody a great deal of embarrassment if I would just quietly withdraw my membership from the church. This left me without a church. I was very concerned about my children's souls. I still sent them to Christian schools, and I asked my mother if she was still praying and to please pray for the souls of my children. But I felt so alone.

"Then I got to thinking: when I was in the church where we were all going to heaven, we hardly talked to each other on earth. How is it that when we hit heaven, in a twinkling of an eye, everything will change? Will everybody start loving and caring up there? Or, in heaven am I still going to feel like an outcast—like I'm never really good enough?

"After they asked me to leave the church, I went to churches—all kinds of different churches. And in every church maybe the minister would say hello to me, if I stood in line. In some churches, maybe a deaconess or a greeter would come up and welcome me. Sometimes—maybe—someone would share a hymnal with me, but when I left the service that was it. It was as though I had entered somebody else's sacred domain, and if I worked really hard—if I went back again and again and again—*maybe* I would find a church family there; but I didn't have the energy to try.

"I was so turned off in every church I went to because nobody cared; nobody cared that I, a human being with feelings and thoughts and emotions, came into their doors. And that is when I went to People's Temple. Everyone seemed so caring and loving. They hugged us and made us welcome. So many people said they liked us and wanted us to come back. After the first service, many people sent letters. The church even sent a box of candy."

Grace Stoen told me a similar story. Her mother was Mexican. Her father was Maltese. She is a beautiful, olive-complected woman. Yet the discrimination she experienced in a white parochial school in San Francisco, because she was poor and not-quite-white, made her feel unloved and uncared for in her church—and a perfect candidate for membership in People's Temple.

"I remember walking into my Catholic school, and the Irish kids would call me nigger," Grace recalled. "When I told my parents, they told me not to listen to them. My mother was a Mexican, and all her life she had been told that Mexicans were dirty and that they were no good. So she worked doubly hard to make sure that we had neat, clean uniforms. But one day when I was in the second grade, I played kickball on the way to parochial school and my shoes got scuffed. A nun

made me stand in front of the class and proceeded
to humiliate me. She said I was filthy, and why
would I come to school like that?

"We lived on the fringe of a very rich parish.
The rich and the white were always favored.
Once in the second grade they expected us kids to
bring envelopes with money in them. We didn't
have any money, but they still asked me why I
didn't put any money in the envelope. I was in the
second grade and being put up for not having
money in my envelope.

"Money was all they talked about. They
wanted people to give fifty dollars. They had
plaques on the wall saying who had given five
hundred dollars and who had given one thousand
dollars. When I was eighteen I still didn't have
five hundred dollars, but I finally realized why it
was that there were all those special memorials
for the people who gave money, but nobody ever
befriended me. I had spent ten years of my life in
that church, one day a week, and I never knew
anybody. I just saw all these family cliques and
the strong white Irish thing. So I quit.

"When I went to People's Temple they still
weren't taking any offerings. I'll never forget seeing all the races, black and white together. You
always heard it couldn't be done, that they could
never get along, yet at the Temple there were
educated people and illiterate. There were middle
class people and poor people. There was every-

thing there, and I was really touched by the warmness of the people. You didn't see people whispering—you know—talking about other people. Everybody was openarmed and getting to know one another, and I felt like my heart was just taken by those beautiful people."

They Didn't Feel Our Churches Cared for the Needy

Al Mills, a chemical technician for Standard Oil for seventeen years, remembers joining his wife's Disciples of Christ Church. "They were building a new church," he told me. "Everyone worked on this big evangelism program, trying to go out and get new members because we had this big debt. It was a large church, and they needed a lot of people to pay the bills, but their program didn't include very much of what Jesus was doing—you know—helping the poor and stuff like that. They were helping themselves.

"So I got involved in a social-action department of the church. There were only a few people that were really interested in social change. Nobody really wanted to do anything. They were happy to listen to your message and thought you did a beautiful job of giving a speech; but as far as taking the time to write a letter to a congressman or to take on some worthy cause, they couldn't get out and do anything. They were good listeners—at least I thought they were good listeners. They may have been asleep!

"Later I became chairman of the social-action department of the Council of Churches in West Contra Costa County. We worked on an open-housing covenant, which was to allow people the opportunity to sign a covenant saying they would accept people into their neighborhood regardless of race, color, or creed. I brought the covenant to my church and only asked that they prayerfully consider signing it. They wouldn't even prayerfully consider it!

"So I joined Jones. He was able to get people to do anything. A lot of people came to Jones out of his social-change program to make this a better world to live in. He was able to get his whole congregation to demonstrate for an issue or write letters against a bill that would be harmful to the poor. And I thought, *Now, this is the type of man that seems to be able to do the things that I had hoped to do but could not, because alone I felt so helpless.*"

Like Al Mills, Tim Stoen's concern for the poor and the discriminated against helped lead him from a Presbyterian church to the People's Temple.

"I was working to make my church more socially responsible, and yet I drove a Porsche and lived a very capitalistic life-style. I felt more and more uneasy about the bridge between the rich and the poor. I saw myself as privileged. I would hear a sermon about a Christian's responsibility for the poor, and then see all the poor blacks on

Fillmore Street and wonder why should this gap between us be allowed. It was wrong that there should be inequality in our society. Everybody was talking but nobody was willing to sacrifice. Nobody was willing to take ridicule. So I started looking for a cause, a community to answer these questions. I was willing to do anything to create a utopian community based on equality. That's when I found Jim Jones.''

Although Wayne Pietila had ''a very religious mother'' and ''grew up in Nazarene Sunday schools,'' he felt he had ''no direction and no goals'' when he first visited People's Temple in Ukiah. ''I was a freshman in high school,'' he told me. ''I had already been in trouble with the law for burglary and was running with a rough crowd at school. I was on probation and even so was starting into drugs when I went to People's Temple. Jones gave me direction. He gave me goals. We were a family.

''My church in Ukiah didn't offer much for kids in those days, and so a lot of us quit going. But at People's Temple there were a lot of teenagers. At our first meeting, we took our shoes off because they were taking care of the carpet. We sat on the floor. It was really friendly. Everybody sat together. You didn't have to sit all stiff listening to somebody preach at you. You just felt loose. You could get up and move around. But when Jim Jones came in and stood up to speak, everybody just fell quiet.

"He didn't talk a lot about religion. He talked about helping the poor and feeding the hungry. He helped us kids organize a free breakfast program. He showed us how to find a house for people, rent it, clean it up, move furniture into it and move them in. They didn't even know about People's Temple. We just did that for people, and it made me feel good."

Clare Bouquet's young son died in Jonestown. Her son's story of his conversion to Jones is similar to Wayne's story. "Bryan never rejected our church; I can't say that he ever said he hated the church or anything like that. He just kind of drifted away, stopped attending mass, and the next thing I knew he was with Jim Jones.

"One day he came home, collected all his stuff and moved to the People's Temple in Ukiah. He was in Los Angeles for about a year after the church moved from Northern California. Then one day he appeared at home again and said, 'I think I'm going to Guyana.'

"I said, 'Oh, dear God. Bryan, please, honey, don't go down there.' I begged him.

"He said, 'Mom, you mean you are so selfish?'

"I was trying to think of excuses to give him other than the fact that I thought Jim Jones was a crook.

"I said, 'Well, honey, I would really miss you at Christmastime.' I was grabbing at straws.

"And he said, 'You mean you are so selfish that you would want me to give up this opportunity of

a lifetime to work in this beautiful paradise because you would miss me at *Christmas?'*

"And I thought, *Boy, did I blow that one.* But
then I asked him to promise me that he wouldn't
go without saying good-bye. So he promised.
'Oh, Mom, I would never do that.' "

One day Bryan Bouquet disappeared into the
Guyanese jungle. Clare Bouquet never stopped
trying to make contact with him and to get him
back. She even flew to Guyana with Congressman Ryan and was in Georgetown when she
heard the terrible news.

Sherwin Harris was also in Georgetown that
night trying to get his daughter, LeAnn, out of the
cult. His wife, Linda Sharon Amos, his daughter,
LeAnn, and his two stepdaughters all died in
Georgetown. Guyanese police are still trying to
determine if the women's throats were slit by
their own hand or by the hand of another cultist.

Linda Sharon Amos came from a Jewish home.
But when I asked her husband about this apparent failure of Protestant, Catholic, and Jewish religions in the Jonestown tragedy, he saw it differently.

"You ask about a failure of religion," he said,
"and at some level there was. But on the other
hand, Jones continuously pandered to the people's sense of altruism and higher ideals instilled
in them by the very religions they rejected. He
didn't go around religious truth or experience. He
told them they were creating a brave new world.

He told them they were the true believers doing true good. And when they had to do horrible things, he explained that these horrible things they did were necessary for the greater good of all. He used the religious message to his own ends. He played upon the very sensitivities instilled in those people by their churches; and by the time people realized where they had gone astray, it was too late.''

Looking back on Jones's techniques, Grace Stoen reflected, ''He took advantage of people who felt unloved and in need. They were either in college or in some transition like divorce or being widowed. Or they were poor with five children or old and on welfare. They would walk into the Temple and five people would immediately step forward to take care of their needs. They would get you a place to live. They would buy you food. They would take care of you in practical ways.''

Al Mills added, ''Jones promised that kind of care for life. He claimed he would provide everything we needed. Our children would be sent to college. We would always have medical care. We would never go hungry. He promised the people everything.''

Several subjects quoted Jones as saying, ''Other churches talk about helping people. I am going to do it.'' This practical caring was good news to people who saw their home churches as uncaring, even cruel. And so the majority of those who came to Jones were the needy ones:

the poor, the discriminated against, the unloved; while the minority of his followers were middle-class, privileged, and joined Jones not out of need but out of need to help the needy. They left their churches and joined the People's Temple because they wanted a chance to love others in practical, effective ways not provided by the churches they knew.

So they came to Jones from our churches. He provided a warm and caring community to those in need who felt rejected by the churches of their past. And for those who felt their churches were uninterested in the poor and disadvantaged, he provided a program for social change. It was a mutually beneficial arrangement. Those who wanted to change the world got their workers, and the workers got their board and room. And Jones led them all to the land of promise, and from the land of promise—into death.

For Reflection and Discussion

1. What do you most need from your church or fellowship group that you are not getting?
2. What gifts do you have that you would like to use to serve your church, but have found no way or encouragement to do so?
3. What needs of others do you believe it is the church's responsibility to meet?
4. What most disillusions you about what you see in your church? other churches?

5. How do you think you'd feel if you came to your church as a newcomer?
6. Consider 1 John 3:7. How does it apply to you, your friends, your church? How does it apply to what people saw when they first came to People's Temple?

Scripture Text

1 John 3:7

Little children, let no one deceive you. He who does right is righteous, as he is righteous.

2

Jones Created an Illusion of Respectability

We are all vulnerable.

As the San Francisco *Chronicle* published its first death list, I drove from Berkeley into the city seeking more insights into why so many of our Christian brothers and sisters were listed. I parked on Geary Boulevard and stared at the three-story People's Temple Christian Church. Once a Masonic Hall, this old building should be preserved as a monument to Christian gullibility. Jones knew all the tricks played in the name of evangelism and church growth, but he twisted and distorted them to suit his own ambition; so, many Christians, whether black, brown, or white, impoverished or middle class, were taken in.

But Jones didn't just fool them. He fooled, deceived, or in some way compromised everyone, from the White House to the City Hall; from the mansions on Nob Hill to the tenements in the Tenderloin, from the Council of Churches to the headquarters of the Disciples of Christ. Before we piece together what Jim Jones did in the dark to enslave and destroy his flock, we need to examine the tricks he played on all of us in the light. Like a contractor who builds a high fence around an ugly hole and covers the fence with bright posters and cheerful greetings, Jim Jones put up a wall of deception that fooled almost everyone.

In the following chapters we'll go behind the wall to visit the haunted house of God he constructed, but before we go, it seems important to stare at the colorful wall of lies that hid the real horror he was building inside.

Walk the streets around the Temple. There a high-rise tenement, waiting to be torn down for urban renewal, houses families of the poor and unemployed. Here a black man leans against a neighborhood tavern, staring at the street. Children play in front of a twenty-four-hour-grocery store with its iron grillwork and inflated prices. A row of Victorian houses stands empty, its welfare renters displaced, so that some young architect with a flare for fixer-uppers can rent them to those who can afford them. Children, old people, mothers with babies line up for buses, as the commuters in their Mercedes roar in from the suburbs. Into the Fillmore district, with its poverty and its fear and its hopelessness, moved Jim Jones.

Jones Knew How to Inspire Hope

The Rev. Jesse Jackson rightly warns us not to overlook the good Jones did in our attempt to understand the bad. Jim Jones, whatever his motives, knew how to give people hope. It wasn't just the exciting, hope-filled worship services he staged with professional orchestras and trained youth choirs. It wasn't just his inspiring, hope-filled sermons. Jones and the hardworking members of the People's Temple also initiated an amazing number of programs to help people in practical ways.

In 1971, Jones's church from Redwood Valley purchased the Albert Pike Masonic Memorial Temple at 1859 Geary Boulevard. Within months the word went out: "Here's a preacher who is trying to help us." As in the late fifties in Indianapolis, Indiana, where Jones opened his first interdenominational church, and in the early sixties in Redwood Valley, California, where he opened his first West Coast Temple, Jones immediately set up showy social-action programs to help the needy. He counseled exprisoners and juvenile delinquents. He started a job-placement center. He opened rest homes and homes for the retarded. In San Francisco he had a health clinic offering free Pap smears and other diagnostic services. He organized a vocational training course and a drug-rehabilitation center and provided free legal aid. His Temple Dining Hall on Geary Boulevard fed from eight hundred to eighteen hundred people a day.

In Redwood Valley, Jones founded a community center with a heated swimming pool, also horses for underprivileged children to ride. There were college dormitories and tuition grants for students. There were homes for seniors; an animal shelter; medical facilities with free diagnoses; an outpatient clinic; a drug-rehabilitation program that gave evidence of curing three hundred addicts; legal aid to two hundred families a month. In short, there was *something for everyone*.

Now reports are surfacing about old people locked in Jones's crowded, filthy "rest homes," drug addicts "beaten and abused," and unnourishing gruel being served in the Temple food line, and even to the people in Guyana. And there is no doubt that Jones promised more than he delivered. Jones used these service projects to advance his power and reputation. Jones created false hope built on lies. But to wipe out all the thousands of hours that the dedicated members put into serving others, to minimize the practical ways Jones and the Temple served people, is to oversimplify the facts and miss a point we Christians need to remember. There are people in great need living all around our churches, in the city *or* in the suburbs. Before we discount Jones's work on their behalf, we should remember how little we are doing to help the needy ones in our own neighborhoods. Jones taught us an important lesson. When you give the people hope in practical ways—even if that hope is built on lies—the people fill the church. No wonder our churches are so empty of the poor, the uneducated, the outcasts—the kind of people Jesus seemed to love the most.

Jones Promoted Himself Through Celebrities

Jones was also a master of public relations. The same black mother on Geary Boulevard, who heard that Jones's Temple provided free medical care for her sick child, also saw endless pictures of Jones in the newspapers with political and entertainment celebrities. She didn't know that Jones was seated at a luncheon beside Mrs. Jimmy Carter because he had ordered Temple members bussed to her appearance, when there had been no time to gather a normal crowd. She didn't know that Governor Jerry Brown hardly knew the man when they were photographed smiling and waving together. She didn't know that Mayor George Moscone appointed Jones to the Commission on Housing because Jones turned out Temple members to campaign house-to-house for him.

I have a picture of myself shaking hands with President Ford. It is a typical example of how this fame by association can work. I was invited to fill an extra place at a White House luncheon. All 150 of the guests were lined up to be photographed, one by one, with the President. When my turn came, I reached out to shake his hand, said, "Hello, I'm glad to . . . ." The strobe flashed, and before I could finish the sentence, a smiling aide guided me gently past the President and to a table where I could place orders for the picture. Now whenever I want to impress my children that their daddy really was a friend of Presidents, I take out the picture and show it grandly.

In the aftermath of Guyana, we are learning how thoroughly Jim Jones understood this fame-by-association technique and how effectively he used it. To prove how widely recommended to them Jones had been, the Guyanese displayed to the press letters commending Jones from Vice-President Walter Mondale; Health, Education and Welfare Secretary Joseph Califano; the late Senator Hubert H. Humphrey; Senators Sam Ervin, Warren Magnuson, Henry Jackson, Philip A. Hart, Mike Gravel, and a host of other members of Congress.

Mondale wrote, "Knowing of the congregation's deep involvement in the major social issues of our country is a great inspiration to me." Califano wrote, "[Mr. Jones's] interest in protecting individual liberty and freedom has made an outstanding contribution to furthering the cause of human dignity." Humphrey wrote, "The work of Rev. Jim Jones and his congregation is testimony to the positive and truly Christian approach to dealing with the myriad problems confronting our society today."

I hope there were no Christians who looked askance at those poor, embarrassed politicians when they learned how carelessly these broad endorsements had been given, because it happens in our Christian world all the time. Millions of Christians pick up whichever books and records are most heavily touted and watch the Christian films and television programs most expensively advertised, never realizing how much they have in common at that moment with the victims of Jonestown. Politicians can hardly avoid being photographed with the corrupt and the ambitious, but we don't have to be taken in by the pictures. Celebrities will go on endorsing products they know little about, but we don't have to believe them. Secular advertising gimmicks continue to seduce those who market Christian goods and services, but we don't have to rush to buy before we discriminate between the good, the bad, and the awful.

Jones Manipulated the Press

Jones knew that public relations demanded cooperation by the press. One bad news story, one thorough investigation by any one of the media could have tumbled his empire. So Jones worked tirelessly to win the press to his side. In September 1976, Jones and a large group from People's Temple put on a public demonstration for the four Fresno, California, newsmen who were jailed for not revealing sources. The Temple contributed forty-four hundred dollars to twelve California newspapers for use "in defense of the free press" and four thousand dollars more to

assist *Los Angeles Times* reporter Bill Farr, who
went to jail for refusing to release the names of his
sources. These were not simply acts of Christian
charity. These were embarrassingly obvious attempts to win the press to his side.

Jones hounded reporters to give the Temple
good stories and had his congregation make hundreds of nuisance calls and send thousands of critical letters to correspondents who seemed determined to write anything that questioned Jones or
the Temple. And the campaign paid off in positive
stories that the innocent victim of Jonestown read
for years in the newspapers of Indianapolis,
Ukiah, and San Francisco.

Forgive me for underlining the obvious, but the
tragedy in Guyana should be a reminder that what
we read in the secular or religious press is written
by people under great pressure to meet deadlines
and budgets and subscription quotas. To be informed is to read widely and critically. Yet we
Christians hardly read any news at all. The few
religious magazines that raise questions and poke
fun at our foibles have little support from the
mass of us. Our denominational papers have almost no investigative reporting, no controversial
letters to the editor, no open forums where many
sides of the crucial issues are discussed. We
probably wouldn't read them anyway. Our local
church papers should have sermon titles and
rummage-sale ads, I suppose, but we could also
write our own or quote others' opinions on local

or national issues that affect us all. We can be grateful that our city newspaper church-page editors have organized to get significant news back on the church page. We should encourage them, even when we don't agree with what they report. They and those like them can help us respond to issues like the People's Temple before it happens again, this time in our town.

It was Lester Kinsolving, an Episcopalian priest and journalist, who sounded the first warning against the Temple in 1972. It was a courageous article in an almost unknown California magazine, *New West* (August 1, 1977), that sent Jones scurrying to Jonestown. And it was a freelance reporter from Ukiah, Kathy Hunter, who pursued the truth about the Temple all the way to Georgetown in May 1978.

Jones Pretended to Be Christian

Jim Jones became a Christian when he was just a child. The biographical fragments available to us agree that Mrs. Myrtle Kennedy, a devout member of the Church of the Nazarene, was influential in young Jones's conversion. According to our source, at fourteen he carried his Bible to school and preached to his classmates, "frightening his listeners with visions of hell, where sinners burn forever."

At about the same time, Jones's father separated from his mother and she and Jimmie moved to Richmond, Indiana. After graduating from high

school at eighteen, Jones married Marceline
(Marcie) Baldwin, a nurse he met in the
Richmond Hospital. He attended Indiana Univer-
sity but quit to preach in Indianapolis and to form
his own church there. When he graduated from
Butler University (with a degree in education)
after ten years of night school, he called himself a
Unitarian; yet the first independent church he
founded, Jones called the Christian Assembly
Church. After two years spent in Belo Horizante,
Brazil, seeking a place to escape the pending nuclear holocaust he predicted, Jim Jones returned
to Indianapolis, affiliated with the Disciples of
Christ, and was ordained by that denomination in
1964.

What happened to Jones in his own private
Christian pilgrimage will probably never be fully
known. The subjects I have interviewed who
knew him from the late sixties in Redwood Valley, where he founded the second Temple, believe he was a complex mix of good and evil, who
let evil get the better of him. Few disagree that by
the time he reached Ukiah in 1965 he was only
pretending to be a Christian, using the language
and forms of faith and his apparent Christian social concern as a means to gaining power and a
place in history.

Over the years Jones became a master in his
use of Christian trappings. On the door above the
Temple in San Francisco, the sign still hangs advertising the People's Temple Christian Church,

affiliated with the Disciples of Christ. On the minister's business card of Michael Prokes, one of Jones's top aides, the church is billed as "a multi-racial, interfaith, human service ministry." And the unsuspecting people who had heard the promises from Jones and his People's Temple, who had read complimentary stories in the San Francisco press, who had seen Jones's picture on television and in the newspapers with the famous and the powerful, knew only that they were entering an allegedly Christian church, affiliated with a respectable denomination, headed by an ordained Christian pastor.

Jones Exploited Christian Worship and Community

I walked up to the door of the Temple, hoping for a chance to see firsthand the sanctuary where Jones and his followers met for those five years in San Francisco. Heavy iron gates blocked my entrance. When I rang the doorbell, no one came to answer. Three well-dressed black men in a white Cadillac Seville parked nearby eyed me suspiciously. A lone police car slowly patrolled the street. There would be no going inside the People's Temple Christian Church that day.

According to researchers from the Spiritual Counterfeits Project, a group of Christians in Berkeley who investigate and write about the cults, the worship services at the Temple featured "fundamentalist-pentecostal Christian trappings and biblical language." People dressed casually. Temple members were friendly and outgoing. There was a time of informal greetings and discussion before the service began.

Jeannie Mills, one of the Temple defectors, still remembers her second visit to the Temple in Redwood Valley. "It was a beautiful group," she told me. "The people there really cared for me as a human being. One of the things that impressed me was their response to my pedigreed dogs. If I told people at work that I had a show Afghan, the daughter of West Winds Gazebo, the most fantastic Afghan in the northern hemisphere, my co-workers would be wowed; but when I told the people at the Temple they said, 'So?' And I thought, *This is great, fantastic; these people don't really care. No longer am I judged by what I have or what I wear,* as I had been all my life. As a child I was judged because I didn't have enough clothes, and then I tried to overcompensate by really putting on a big show. Then I was judged by that. But at the Temple all of a sudden I was with a group of people who worried about what I thought. They wanted to know where I was coming from. And they wanted to share life experiences with me. It was a whole new world and I loved it."

All the subjects I interviewed remember especially how the interracial dimension of Temple worship impressed them when they entered. Mills continues, "No thunder and lightning clapped when black and white people touched and got close together. It was wonderful." After greeting informally, the crowd began to sing foot-stomping gospel music mixed with freedom songs from the sixties: "Oh, Freedom," "We Shall Overcome," "Black Baby," and the like. The people grabbed hands or put their arms around each other and sang and swayed with the music.

After the music came a time of testimony, with people reporting on what God was doing in their lives through Jones's ministry. By the time Jones came out, the enthusiastic band and professional music by the choirs, the loud, happy singing by the congregation, and the time of praise and testimony had created a warm, loving atmosphere. Into the midst of this worship service, Jones would come, leading music, reading from the newspapers stories of noteworthy interest, prophesying directly to strangers in the congregation, preaching and healing.

One visitor to the Temple remembers that on his visit there, "After the singing, Jones appeared, wearing sunglasses and a red robe. During his long sermon, a woman collapsed near the front of the church. After the ushers pronounced her dead, Jones laid hands on her and prayed, whereupon she appeared to have been revived. Jones then claimed to have raised her from the dead; most of the congregation seemed to accept this claim at face value." During the service, Jones's primary claim and message was that he was God's messenger, sent "to make God real to people."

Now, of course, we are certain that the prophecies and miracles were totally contrived. Chicken parts were displayed as cancers removed miraculously from dying bodies. Spies were sent from the congregation to the homes of visitors to collect information on the unsuspecting seeker that Jones would integrate into his personalized prophecies. People who "died" and were revived "miraculously" in the service were Jones's close associates in elaborate disguises, each one new for the occasion. These farces were so carefully created that even the church photographer, Al Mills, now a Temple defector, and Tim Stoen, the second most powerful man in the Temple, did not realize they were faked.

Jones Exported Christian Worship and Community

I walked to the rear of the Temple where Jones's buses are still parked alongside automobiles donated by his grateful flock and large shipping crates stamped FOR THE PEOPLE'S TEMPLE, GEORGETOWN, GUYANA. In those buses, people from the Temple commuted every week to Los Angeles to hold services, first in rented auditoriums, and then in a large hall he purchased there. Jones rode the four hundred miles from San Francisco in a private, bullet-proof bus complete with bed and bathroom; while hundreds of his followers were forced to accompany him in crowded buses of their own.

In Los Angeles, Jones and his troop created miracle services for the poor and the needy who lived in the deteriorating heart of the city. A locked and secret compartment of Jones's bus was filled with wigs, makeup, crutches, and phony cancers. The people needed hope and healing. Through his so-called miracles he gave them both. And the people gave him money and power in return.

Though Jones is dead, the needs that made people vulnerable to him still haunt the inner city. As our mainline churches move to the suburbs, itinerant evangelists and faith healers move in to take their place. They all rent auditoriums. They all advertise miracle services. They all provide instant though short-lived Christian community. And how are the people who flock to their crusades to discriminate between those who are genuine and those who are not?

Now television is carrying this peculiar miracle phenomenon from the city to the suburbs and across the nation, and we are all left with the problem of discriminating between what is genuine and what is not.

I am not impugning the integrity of any evangelist or healer holding miracle services or television crusades, but I have attended and watched these miracle meetings for years. To the best of my knowledge, no church or interchurch commission, no local, state, or federal agency, and no media association even monitors any of these miracle workers. The miracles are checked only by those who perform them. The money collected at the services is likewise gathered, with those taking it being accountable to no one. As it was in Jones's day, it is today. *The scene is perfect for breeding others like him.* Potential victims, in their innocence and need, line up to be exploited.

All of us are vulnerable. Open your mail box. Turn on your television set. Pick up any religious magazine or newspaper. For five dollars a month you can do anything from winning the world for God through a satellite to feeding the world's poor or healing the world's sick. Some of the promises are true. Some are half-true. Some are lies. All of the promises oversimplify. Most exaggerate. Jones knew it didn't matter. Make the promises loud enough and long enough, and too many gullible Christians will rush to believe. No one asks to see if the promises are really kept. No one asks to see the financial records.

It was the press who finally uncovered the truth about Jones and his promises. That is why he had worked so hard and spent so much money keeping them deceived. Must we depend on the press or the government agencies to regulate the church? Or should we take responsibility to regulate ourselves, to check out the promises of miracles and those who make them?

It is all too easy to set up the miracle services and telecast them to the world. It is easy to buy full-page ads in the Friday *Times* to promise the people anything. It is easy to be photographed with or endorsed by some unwitting Christian celebrity. And it is easy to manipulate the press or avoid it altogether. But what awful price do people pay? The trucks pull out of town. The television screens grow dark. Then people are left to deal with reality, without the miracle they had been promised.

Of all the illusions Jim Jones created, this promise of miracles surrounded by the trappings of a warm, loving, Christian community was the most insidious. For the unwary poor who needed hope; for the sick and dying, reaching out for help and healing; for the unsuspecting young person, tired of boredom in the churches and ready to work; for the visiting political dignitary or celebrity who saw only these carefully staged productions, Jones's miracle services were the most effective camouflage of all.

As I sat staring at the Temple, the sound of two thousand worshipers singing "What a Mighty God We Serve" echoed in my brain. I imagined them black and white together, arm in arm, tears streaming down their faces, or laughing and clapping and dancing for joy; and I hated Jones for this deception more than all the rest; for the bodies of those same worshipers were at that very moment being unloaded from the cavernous holds of C–141 military air transports. In shiny aluminum coffins, whole families of them were being delivered to a military morgue in Delaware. Jones lured them to the Temple with his illusion of God's miracle, and they died never knowing what God can really do to set us free! Then again, where were we when the victims of Jonestown needed us? And what can we do right now to guarantee we will not be deceived again?

For Reflection and Discussion

1. On what sources of information do you most rely? Where could you go to get other points of view?
2. How would you react to your church, if you were coming for the first time and were a member of another race? if you were destitute?
3. Compare John 4:48 and 2 Timothy 3:5. Do you think we should deny hope of the miraculous to protect ourselves from false hope? Why or why not?
4. Read Jeremiah 17:9, 1 Corinthians 3:18, and 2 Corinthians 11:13–15. How do they relate to each other? to us? to Jones's success?

Scripture Texts

John 4:48
Jesus therefore said to him, "Unless you see signs and wonders you will not believe."

2 Timothy 3:5
Holding the form of religion but denying the power of it. Avoid such people.

Jeremiah 17:9
The heart is deceitful above all things, and desperately corrupt; who can understand it?

1 Corinthians 3:18
Let no one deceive himself. If any one among you thinks he that is wise in this age, let him become a fool that he may become wise.

2 Corinthians 11:13–15
For such men are false apostles, deceitful workmen, disguising themselves as apostles of Christ. And no wonder, for even Satan disguises himself as an angel of light. So it is not strange if his servants also disguise themselves as servants of righteousness. Their end will correspond to their deeds.

3

Jones Killed Their Faith in the Bible and the Church

The Abuse of Authority

It was fairly simple for Jim Jones to con and persuade the outside general public with his exaggerated claims about the Temple's good works; his manipulation of the press; his constant association with the powerful and famous; his growing political clout and his well-staged miracle services. But the indoctrination of his army of followers was a much more insidious and complex procedure. It began at the door of the Temple. There were special services staged to impress and deceive the outsiders that almost anyone could attend. But on the average day, even getting into the Temple was no easy task.

On the death list from Guyana you will find the name *David G*. Grace Stoen remembers the first time he came to the People's Temple Church in San Francisco. "David had been on drugs," she told me. "He was often high and never held down a job. He had gotten a woman pregnant, and one Sunday, David, his wife, and baby came to church. But the people who guarded the doors would not let him in. They let his wife and daughter in but kept David out. He fought and screamed and pounded on the door. He tried for weeks and weeks to get in. Finally he made it. I think he died in Guyana.''

He Picked His Victims Carefully

Jones set up a screening process to keep out potential troublemakers or critics, and let in people most likely to be vulnerable to his influence. Obviously, the screening measures were rigorously enforced. Grace Stoen describes them this way: ''We used to have to screen people at the door. We would ask people their names, telephone numbers, occupations and everything, before they got in. If you were white and educated, with a profession or anything to do with churches, you were heavily screened. Jones found out early that religious people were his best workers, but not ministers or church leaders. They were really skeptical of white people. In fact, the majority of the people that they let in were black people who were religious and in need.

''If you got past the door screening,'' she continued, ''you were sat down in a room and maybe three people talked to you. They would ask different questions such as 'What do you think of integration?' or, 'What do you think of God?' and if you didn't give the right answers, you were asked to leave."

There were exceptions. Tim Stoen, the young lawyer who became Jones's number 2 man; Al Mills, and other professionals who were also white and educated got into the Temple because they were needed by Jones for specialized tasks. How he ensnared these exceptional cases and kept them loyal to the People's Temple, we will consider later.

As soon as one entered the Temple, the undermining of one's old beliefs began. What I am about to describe as Jones's "brainwashing" techniques may not have been applied to everyone in exactly the same way; nor were the techniques necessarily the same in the early days in Indianapolis as in the later days in San Francisco. I don't know if Jones's strategy was as self-conscious or as systematic as it will sound when I try to describe it; but the same kinds of tricks are consistently mentioned in interviews with my subjects, and I am simply trying to outline them to help us understand how it was done.

The first problem Jones had to overcome was the problem of *authority*. Visitors came to the Temple believing in varying degrees that God, the Bible, and the churches of their childhood were trustworthy. Whether traditional beliefs were held consciously or unconsciously, the thoughts and actions of the potential members were conditioned by the Ten Commandments, the teachings of Jesus, and the theological and ethical teachings of their churches. It was Jones's most important task to eliminate the people's confidence in God, the Bible, and their churches, and to insert himself into the position of ultimate authority in their lives.

He Used Positive Appeals

We can put these authority-transfer techniques in the categories of positive appeals and disillusioning attacks. As people passed through the screening process at the door and outer conference rooms of the Temple, the positive appeals began. Al Mills remembers his first visit to the Temple in Redwood Valley. "The first meeting we went to, we had just gotten off a bus, and a woman came up to us and said that Pastor Jim Jones had healed her of terminal cancer. [Later I learned that she was Linda Sharon Amos, the woman whose throat was cut in Guyana and a very important member of Jones's inner staff.] On our way in people would come up to us and say all these wonderful things about Pastor Jim Jones."

Apparently the hard-core workers were sent out to prepare the potential members with these commercials for Jones's power and trustworthiness—even before the service began. Inside the church there were more testimonies to Jones, more "soft-sell" conditioning as a part of Temple worship. Mills remembers that "people would stand up in line to tell what Pastor Jones had done for them. One said, 'Pastor Jones had a revelation that saved me and my whole family from an accident that would have killed us.' Another testified, 'My house caught on fire and just the thought of Jones put the fire out.'

"They also had a fantastic singer leading songs of freedom crying out for the society to change: 'Blowing in the Wind,' 'We Shall Overcome,' the [civil rights] songs we sang in Selma. He sang 'My Little Black Baby' and told how Jones had been discriminated against because he had adopted this little black child. Things like that," Mills remembers, "were a part of almost every service."

Later, Mills illustrated how far Jones promoted this seduction by his people of potential Temple members. "People who were religious and believed in Jones's healings would do these tours with Jones, like down to San Francisco and later to Los Angeles, and across the USA. At the evangelism tours where he would demonstrate his healing power, members would stand up and yell in a meeting, 'What manner of man can do these things?' And someone else would answer, 'God Almighty!' "

A part of the authority transfer process was facilitated outside the church with people who hadn't even attended a service yet. "Any time you went shopping in the store," continued Mills, "you were supposed to say to the manager, 'My pastor, Jim Jones, thinks you are running a very reputable place here. He thinks you are a nice person and he urges all of us to shop here.' Well, you know what this does to a guy that is running a business. He begins to think, 'This Jones is quite a wonderful guy.' '' Add to that the constant publicity about the Temple's "good works"; Jones's picture in the paper with other famous people; Jones's growing reputation as a miracle worker and prophet; and it gets easier to see how people could be taken in.

Mills remembers sitting in that first service after all of these persuasive testimonials. "Jones wasn't up on the podium yet, and I began to get this feeling that all of a sudden he would just appear. I hadn't seen him go up to the stage and all of a sudden, as I expected, he was there. I was so engrossed in what was going on and what they were saying about him, that I hadn't even seen him walk up to the side and sit down."

He Used Disillusioning Attacks

When Jones "materialized" in the service, techniques immediately shifted to negative, disillusioning ones. Jeannie Mills remembers that same first meeting in the Redwood Valley Temple.

"In the first sermon I heard him preach," she recalls, "Jones said there were errors in the Bible. I thought to myself, *You can't say that about the Bible*, but he went on to quote errors from the Bible. He took the Bible, threw it on the floor and shouted up at God, 'If there is a God in heaven, strike me dead.' "

Mrs. Mills continued, "I waited—seriously—
for him to get struck dead. I watched him. You
don't say those things to God. Yet God didn't
strike him dead and I was crushed. I was literally
crushed. I never tested it," she explained, "but I
just knew way deep down inside me you don't say
those things. It was as though someone pulled the
rug out from under me and there I was. God failed
me. The Bible was no longer the paragon of
strength I thought it was and I was completely
washed out. I didn't know what to believe. So at
that point I was very susceptible to believe what
this very strong, loving, charismatic person and
these three hundred brand-new friends who loved
me dearly, said for me to believe."

In San Francisco, Grace Stoen recalls that
"Jones did everything slowly. 'Slow change can
occur.' " She quoted Jones as saying, " 'Drastic
change cannot occur.' " She remembers how "he
started attracting these very religious black
people into the church . . . who spoke in tongues
in their churches . . . . At first he went on and
on about the Bible and they really dug it. He got
them in by speaking all the religious words. Then
slowly he would bring up one error in the Bible
and he would say, 'Let's talk about it.' Some
people would get hostile. Some people would
leave and never come back. But some people
stuck by it. Then he would progressively get more
and more unreligious and he would say, 'You

people read the Bible. You talk this and you talk that,' he'd say, 'but, by God, I'm going to do it. I'm going to physically carry out helping people.' That's what I really liked about the Temple,'' concluded Stoen. "We didn't just *talk* about the Bible, but we did what the Bible told us to do. Jones was right in one way. Talk is cheap but actions are costly."

Jeannie Mills was so shocked by the notion that there could be contradictions or questions of agreement in the Bible that she went home, researched and wrote "The Letter Killeth, But the Spirit Giveth Life." She said, "I outlined every error in the Bible I could find. It took that for me to believe there really are errors in the Bible," she explained. "I wanted to make sure for myself." This was Jones's material and he distributed the booklet widely.

"That's the bad thing about religion that is based on the Bible being all true," concluded Al Mills, "because someone like Jones comes along and shows you there are errors in it. If you base your whole truth on the fact the Bible is all true and somebody can prove to you there are errors in it, there goes your faith."

In spite of Jones's attack on Scripture, he never quit using the Bible where it suited and supported him. In fact, in the pavilion in Jonestown where he and his followers died, the verse from 2 Corinthians 3:17 (KJV) hung in a place of honor: WHERE THE SPIRIT OF THE LORD IS, THERE IS LIB-

ERTY. Jones loved to quote such passages describing the first-century church from the Book of Acts as, "They had all things in common," or the words of Jesus, "Sell all you have and come, follow me."

Jones broadened his attacks from the Bible to religion in general. Al Mills told me, "Jones taught that King James was a slave master and that the slaves were brought into the country under the guise of religion. He would tear down religion. 'If there is a God up there,' he used to say, 'why would there be so many starving people in the world? Why would he let some people come into the world lame and let others live such healthy lives?' "

Though Jones saw himself as a reincarnation of Jesus, even Jesus was attacked by Jones. "Jones pointed out that Jesus didn't die for your sins," Mills said. "He didn't bear your cross. You have to bear your own cross in life. He would talk about how Jesus in the end actually denied the loving God Himself with His words *Why hast thou forsaken me?* In the very end Jesus Himself weakened."

And under this attack many were deceived. When I asked Mills if everyone had been so easily taken in, he answered, "The minute that some people saw him throw the Bible down, they broke away. It was too much for them. So these people would go away. They weren't people he wanted anyway. He had a process of drawing in, breaking down, and reeducating. He let those that fell away, fall away; and those that stayed became so caught up in it and so compromised they couldn't leave. If he was successful in breaking down their beliefs in the Bible and breaking down their beliefs in Jesus, then they would stay in.''

He Put Himself in Jesus' Place

Once this breaking down of faith in the old authorities took place, Jones replaced the God of Israel with himself, Jim Jones. Wayne Pietila, who joined the cult as a youngster, remembers that Jones seemed gradually to see himself as God's replacement. ''Jim Jones was like a father to me,'' he remembers. ''I could go to him when I had problems, talk to him, and he always understood. I lived with him anytime I wanted. I could just drive up to his house in Redwood Valley and talk to him. But as the years went by, he became colder to the individual needs of the people and started wanting himself put upon a pedestal like God.

''In 1973 he actually came out and said he wanted to be called *Father*, and he wanted us to pray to him. He wanted us to carry around his picture in our wallets. I couldn't do that. He had little healing cloths that he would anoint and everyone had to carry them. We had to meditate for two minutes when we got in our cars, so we wouldn't have an accident.''

Jean Mills describes her feelings at that same

time in 1973. "Up to that time we loved him. We would follow him because he was a really neat guy. He was our buddy. We would sit in his house with him and talk to him. You could joke with him then. He was a neat, neat person. But in 1973 he turned into 'Father' and you couldn't confront him anymore."

By then Jones had developed an effective though theatrical system to prove his claims to be their new "god." And because so many of his victims had been accustomed to responding unthinkingly to prophecies and miracles in their own religious traditions, he fooled them to the end. Al Mills remembers Jones calling out his name from the platform during the second service they attended. "He called us up and said, 'I see a little red wagon and it says such and such on the side of it. There's something defective in the steering mechanism of the wagon and you had better check it in a hurry.' He also said we had a dog and that he was fearful of the dog having an accident. He said he saw us in a vision near a French cookbook and named several other details about our home.

"Well, after the service we went straight home and checked his prophecies. And sure enough there was something wrong with the wagon. And our dog did eventually have an accident. He got his ear caught in a rock tumbler in the basement. And near the kitchen window my wife had a cookbook called *La Cuisine de France*.

We were impressed.

"It wasn't until years later we found out that when we gave our name and address at the front door of the Temple, his people were dispatched to our house to survey it, talk to neighbors, rummage through the garbage cans, and look in our windows for clues to information about us."

Wayne Pietila told me, "Day and night we listened to Jones's revelations. One night I'll never forget we were sitting in the church after midnight and Jones said, 'There's going to be proof of the coming atomic holocaust at 3:09 A.M. this morning.' We waited. And exactly at 3:09 A.M. the air-raid siren went off at the Redwood Valley Fire Department. It wasn't the fire signal but the *air-raid* signal. Everybody went, 'Wow!' And Jones said it was our sign to know that what he said would happen. And nobody that was a Temple member really questioned it."

Now the mystery behind Jones's so-called prophecies and miracles has been solved. The world's press has described in vivid detail many of Jones's techniques for working miracles. Apparently, his wife, Marcie, a registered nurse, and a dozen or so staff members were his willing aides in the deception. Jones would approach a victim during his worship service and shout, "This man is dying of cancer," or he would point to parts of the auditorium, place his hand over his face as though having a great "revelation" and cry out, "Someone out there is suffering from a terrible case of arthritis [or emphysema]." Many cases were simply "cured" without evidence. For others, he had devised a mixture of chicken entrails and animal or human blood. He had tiny portions of this rotting mixture in plastic bags which he could pop into a victim's mouth and then successfully remove; or for more elaborate "healings," Marcie accompanied people into the rest room, where an enema was administered and this ugly portion of chicken innards placed in the discharge. The mass was then brought back into the congregation and revealed with, "Stand back, this is deadly cancer." And the people would cheer and praise Jones for his power.

Now with hindsight, it is difficult to believe that so many people were taken in, yet the belief in healing, ancient and biblically based, is held in various ways throughout the entire Christian church. Catholic and Protestant clergymen pray the prayer of faith over the sick and dying. Laymen and women have prayer meetings for healing in churches, homes, and hospitals across the land. Well-recognized evangelists point to a section of an auditorium and claim people "out there" have been miraculously healed by God. Television evangelists claim similar healings for people "out there" in Duluth or San Diego. So why should we find it so difficult to understand how Jones, an ordained Disciples of Christ minister, should be so easily believed? Especially when he faked his cures with such attention to detail. Al Mills admits with some chagrin, "I was the church photographer. I took pictures of those healings. I got people to fill out testimony sheets. I gradually became aware that there were some phony healings, but I still think that many of them were real."

Everyone interpreted the prophecies and the healings differently. Most people were fooled and thousands replaced their faith in God and the Scripture with faith in Jim Jones. At least 912 of them died in the jungle, still calling this imposter *Father*. It is terrible to think how easily people who grew up in our Sunday schools and churches were tricked. But it is even more perplexing to think how quickly they were deceived.

Remember, as was mentioned earlier, Mrs. Mills worked as a teacher in her church for fifteen years. She had studied and taught the Bible in her Seventh Day Adventist Church. Her pastor even wanted her to be trained further to be a full-time Bible worker, yet when I asked her how long it took for her former religious belief to be totally undermined and her new beliefs at the Temple to be totally affirmed, she answered without hesitation, "About a month."

Jones had one purpose in his positive appeals and his disillusioning attacks. He wanted to gain people's exclusive loyalty. Tim Stoen remembers how it happened to him. "I had a vision in my own mind of what a true Christian was; and a true Christian was somebody that was pretty much like Jones. He was like a prophet in the wilderness. He had his excesses and he wasn't very cultured, but I was fascinated with his volcanic energy and that he lived at the level of the people. I had certain criteria in my mind about how I would judge a leader, and one of them was, does he live at the level of the people, or does he leave the meeting before it ends to go and do his own thing? Does he get in his Cadillac afterwards? Jones, even to the end, seemed to have a solicitous concern for his people. He would never leave; he was always the first at the meeting and the last to leave. Afterward I concluded that it was his need to establish and maintain great dependencies on him, but then I needed a sort of God-figure or an authority figure in my life, so I think I just replaced Jesus Christ with Jim Jones . . . ."

That was the first stage of Jim Jones's deception. He destroyed their confidence in the Bible. He pointed out the flaws in their Christian churches. And he took the place of Jesus as the central authority in their lives.

For Reflection and Discussion

1. What initially drew you to your church? Was it a pastor you liked, admired, found interesting or exciting? a particular understanding of Christian truth? Something else?

2. What place does the Bible play in your own faith? If you have confidence in it, what do you think could shake that confidence? On the following

page is a partial list of Bible "errors." How would you have handled this?

3. What does your church teach about the Bible's authority? (If you don't know, find out!)

4. What does the Bible itself teach about its own authority? (*See* 2 Timothy 3:16, 17; 2 Peter 1:20, 21.)

5. Some people protected themselves from Jones by simply leaving when their beliefs were threatened. What are the merits of this tactic? the risks? Consider Romans 16:17, 18 and 2 Corinthians 4:2.

Scripture Text

2 Timothy 3:16, 17

All scripture is inspired by God and profitable for teaching, for reproof, for correction, and for training in righteousness, that the man of God may be complete, equipped for every good work.

2 Peter 1:20, 21

First of all you must understand this, that no prophecy of scripture is a matter of one's own interpretation, because no prophecy ever came by the impulse of man, but men moved by the holy Spirit spoke from God.

Romans 16:17, 18

. . . take note of those who create dissensions and difficulties, in opposition to the doctrine which you have been taught; avoid them. For such persons do not serve our Lord Christ, but their own appetites, and by fair and flattering words they deceive the hearts of the simple-minded.

2 Corinthians 4:2

We have renounced disgraceful, underhanded ways; we refuse to practice cunning or to tamper with God's word, but by the open statement of the truth we would commend ourselves to every man's conscience in the sight of God.

ERRORS

(from "The Letter Killeth, But the Spirit Giveth Life")

MAN WAS CREATED AFTER THE BEASTS AND BEFORE THE BEASTS

> Gen. 1:25, 26: "And God made the beast of the earth after his kind . . . And God said, Let us make man in our image."

> Gen. 2:18–20: "And the Lord God said, It is not good that man should be alone . . . And out of the ground the Lord God formed every beast of the field."

NOAH TOLD BY THE LORD TO TAKE TWO OF EACH BEAST INTO THE ARK, AND ALSO SEVEN

> Gen. 7:2: "Of every clean beast thou shalt take to thee by sevens"

> Gen. 7:8, 9: "Of clean beasts, and of beasts that are not clean . . . There went in two and two"

ABRAHAM HAD ONLY ONE SON, ABRAHAM HAD TWO SONS

> Heb. 11:17: "By faith Abraham . . . offered up Isaac . . . his only begotten son."

> Gal. 4:22: "For it is written that Abraham had two sons"

KETURAH WAS ABRAHAM'S WIFE, OR ABRAHAM'S CONCUBINE?

Gen. 25:1: "Then Abraham took a wife, and her name was Keturah"

1 Chron. 1:32: "Keturah, Abraham's concubine"

GOD PROMISES ABRAHAM EVERYTHING, AND GIVES HIM NOTHING

Gen. 15:8: "And I will give unto thee (Abraham) and to thy seed after thee . . . all the land of Canaan for an everlasting possession."

Acts 7:5: "And he gave him none inheritance in it, no, not so much as to set his foot on."

Heb. 11:9–13: "By faith he sojourned in the land of promise . . . These all died in faith, not having received the promises."

AARON DIED ON MOUNT HOR, AARON DIED IN MOSERA

Num. 33:37–42: "And Aaron the priest went up into Mount Hor at the commandment of the Lord, and died there."

Deut. 10:6, 7: "And the children of Israel took their journey from Beeroth . . . to Mosera: there Aaron died, and there he was buried"

GOD SAYS YOU MUST NOT KILL, HE COMMANDS TO KILL

Ex. 20:13: "Thou shalt not kill"

Ex. 32:27: "Thus saith the Lord God of Israel, put every man his sword by his side, and go in and out from gate to gate throughout the camp, and slay every man his brother"

4

Jones Kept Them in a State of Exhaustion

The Abuse of Time

At the heart of Jones's next step in the deception of so many of our brothers and sisters was his use and abuse of their time. At first I stood in awe of Jones's apparent ability to break down and replace old belief systems so speedily. When Jeannie Mills told me that it took "only about a month" for her former religious beliefs to be "totally undermined" and her new beliefs at the Temple to be "totally affirmed," I could hardly believe it. But after she described to me what happened in a typical Temple month, the speed and effectiveness of Jones's brainwashing was easier to understand.

Time Spent for "Worship" and Instruction

Mrs. Mills remembers well the typical weekly schedule at People's Temple in Redwood Valley. "Sunday there was always a meeting from eleven A.M. to three P.M.," she explained. "We would meet again from six P.M. until approximately three or four A.M. on Monday. Then we would all go to work, sleeping when and if we could. The Planning Commission (which included well over one hundred people) met on Monday nights from seven P.M. until about seven A.M. the next morning. Wednesday night there was a meeting that lasted from seven P.M. until at least two or three A.M. on Thursday morning. Friday night there was a meeting in San Francisco that lasted from seven P.M. until about one A.M. Then we got onto one of the eleven Greyhound buses and drove to Los Angeles (which took at least seven hours); and we would try to sleep as we rode.

"We would arrive in Los Angeles in time for the two P.M. afternoon meeting, which lasted until about six P.M. We would have dinner. The next meeting would start at seven thirty P.M. and last until at least one or two A.M. We would assemble after that public meeting for a planning session that lasted the rest of the night until about eight A.M. in the morning. Our Sunday service would go from eleven A.M. until four P.M., and we would then ride back to Redwood Valley in time to go to school or work the next day."

Not only did Temple members attend endless meetings, but Jones spoke endlessly at most of them. Al Mills remembers the first meeting he attended with his wife at the Redwood Valley Temple. "They had a big banquet between services, and we were enjoying trying to talk to some of the people there, but it got to the point that you couldn't even carry on a conversation because he [Jones] would break in with some revelation or something, or had some announcement to make, and everyone had to shush like that when he talked.''

Jones insisted upon completely dominating the meetings. Either he or his teachings were being praised in word and song, or he was teaching or exhorting the people himself. Jeannie Mills gave an extraordinary example of Jones's tenacity. ''He had to have total, complete, continuous control,'' she said. ''At our Planning Commission meetings, he didn't even take time out to urinate; so his assistant Larry Layton [now under arrest for the murder of Ryan and his party in Guyana] would bring in the can and he would have two nurses hold up a sheet. He would relieve himself and keep talking, while Layton took the can away.''

Just to illustrate how much time Jones spent influencing the beliefs of his followers, compare how much time you have spent in church in the past ten years. If you have averaged two hours a week in worship or study you have been exposed to roughly a thousand hours of content time. Subtract time lost passing around the attendance sheets, listening to announcements, taking offerings, getting ''settled down,'' catching up with last week's lesson, drinking punch or eating cookies (as well as time lost to vacations, illnesses, or just playing hooky) you will be fortunate to have spent five hundred hours in ten years in increasing your Christian education at church. Jones had that much time to influence members of the Temple every ten weeks.

Time Spent Learning to "Survive"

At first the content of Jones's nonstop tirade was his tortured vision of the coming nuclear holocaust. Tim Stoen describes that period in Jones's teaching. "When I first joined the Temple, he talked about nuclear war. He saw it as inevitable. He taught us that there would have to be some sort of remnant that was very disciplined. He was determined to teach us survival skills so that we could recreate the utopian society out of the nuclear wreckage."

Stoen was practicing law in San Francisco and commuting up to Redwood Valley at the time, but Wayne Pietila was just a teenager when Jones was preaching about the holocaust. "He told us that our country was heading for destruction. People's Temple was going to be a family that survived. We stored food in five gallon cans. Rice, grain, even water was sealed in old Chlorox bottles.

"Jones had moved from Indiana," explained Pietila, "because *Esquire* magazine predicted that in the case of a nuclear war, the Ukiah Valley in California would be a naturally protected area. Jet air streams would take the waste right over us and the constant air updraft would carry radioactivity right out of the valley."

So besides the almost endless services and teaching sessions members were forced to attend, they had to prepare for survival as well. "Jones didn't just talk about the end of the earth," remembered Pietila. "In those early years he took all the youth on two camping trips to Oregon out in the wilderness. He helped us build rafts on a river that had rapids. He stuck little kids on them, until they were overloaded. Then he went with us, floating down the rapids for miles, just about to the ocean. Then we hiked the distance back. We picked berries. It was cold at night. We had to wear the same pants constantly. If they got wet you couldn't change them."

So in those early days the congregation spent many hours in preparing to survive the coming nuclear holocaust, and in the later days, to survive the jungle outpost they might soon inhabit. Tim Stoen explains the change in emphasis in the early seventies. "Jones's teaching shifted from the nuclear holocaust concern to a fascist concern. Those were the years Jack Anderson was writing that Nixon might call off the 1972 elections. Jones would say, 'Maybe we err on the side of paranoia, but look what the Jews failed to do when the handwriting was on the wall in Germany under Hitler. It is better to be prepared for this than not.' "

Jones began to dream of building a place where people could live after this nation fell to some kind of fascist despotism. Jean Mills remembers,

"It wasn't Jonestown yet; it was Africa. Then it was Peru. Then finally it was Jonestown." So, the already exhausted people gathered supplies, trained in survival, and prepared to pioneer the new land. Daphene Mills, a teenager, comments that in Redwood Valley, besides attending the teaching and the survival training, she even went to Jones-sponsored Swahili classes to learn to speak to villagers in the African jungle.

Daphene remembers, "It was fun in those days." Similarly, Wayne Pietila recalls, "It was exciting. I still have fond memories of those times. You had a purpose." Many of the people I interviewed look back with melancholy on those "purposeful days" in the Temple, even with the perspective of Jonestown and the massacre of 912 of their friends and neighbors who went all the way to that "new land" they were preparing to build together.

Time Spent Serving Others

In Appendix 4 you will find a visitor report sheet used in the Redwood Valley Temple entitled "A Report of My Visit to a Hungry or Lonely Person." Members were expected to fill out and turn in the complete details of their visits to the needy on a regular basis. The members of Jones's Temple didn't just *visit* the needy. They worked day and night to help the poor, the lonely, the unemployed, drug addicts, exconvicts, the old and the retarded. Anyone in need was seen as their responsibility.

Jones quoted Jesus, the Old Testament prophets, Marx and Lenin, and the social activists of the sixties to motivate his followers to social action. However, it was Jones's teaching of reincarnation that many remember as the primary impetus to their social concern. Wayne Pietila summarized what many now recall as Jones's central teaching of this Eastern notion. "Jones told us we would reap what we sow," he said. "The good deeds we do now would benefit us in the later life. The bad things are going to come back and we will have to pay for them."

Whatever reasons they had motivating them to service, Temple members gave tirelessly to help others. And the subjects I interviewed remember those days of service as exciting and happy—as well as exhausting—days. Grace Stoen remembers tutoring children and tending a houseful of them. Jean and Al Mills ran a Temple rest home and also kept as many as a dozen needy children in their own home. Wayne Pietila fixed up houses and moved poor people into them. The Temple paid the rent. Tim Stoen was one of several Temple attorneys who provided free legal aid to the poor.

Bonnie Thielmann, a daughter of Assembly of God missionaries to Brazil and a defector from the Temple who flew to Guyana with Congressman Ryan's group, recalls her first impressions of the Temple. "On my first visit to Redwood Valley, they took me to see the ranch for retarded children and four or five homes for senior citizens. They were filled with old, black people whom no one else would care for. There were also dormitories for exdrug addicts. There were even animals—a zoo. Anytime anybody in Ukiah wanted to get rid of their animals, they just dropped them off at the People's Temple and Jim fed them all.''

We asked Bonnie how much of the services provided by People's Temple was real, and if the humanitarian work went on in America up to the last days of Jonestown. She replied, "Yes, they were real and, yes, they went on and go on even today. "After I defected from the Temple," she told us, "I called two old black women, friends of mine, Ever Rejoicing and Lovelight, at least once a month. I know that People's Temple was feeding them. Lovelight was going blind, went into the hospital for an operation for her eyes, and the Temple paid for the successful surgery.''

The Temple developed a wide reputation for the good it did. And the work was political as well as social. Mrs. Wayne Boynton, former chairman of the Mendocino County Republicans, told a *Los Angeles Times* correspondent, "They [the Temple members] were a dream come true. They would do precinct work. They would get information from the courthouse. They would do the grubbies—addressing envelopes, making phone calls. They'd do anything you'd ask and so quickly you couldn't believe it."

Linda Dunn, a former member of Jones's "inner staff" of female aides, explained how the Temple did the job so quickly. "We stayed up all night," she said. "Jim wanted us to have as much influence as we could." The pattern is plain. The people exhausted themselves in service and Jones used their hard work to gain power and influence for himself.

Time Spent in Temple Management

As Jones's work load increased, he appointed three support groups to do his bidding: the staff, the Planning Commission, and the counselors. The staff has been described by all the defectors we interviewed as being composed of Jones's most powerful aides and personal harem. The approximately twelve members of this inner staff, most of them women, seemed to set no limits on the evil acts they would perform for Jones. In the early years, the staff assisted him with his miracles and prophecies. Staff members became extremely skilled at feigning illnesses and death, only to be healed or raised from the dead by their boss and co-conspirator. Other staff members went to the homes of Temple visitors, rummaged through garbage cans, and peered in windows to prepare the complex list of personal items upon which Jones based his so-called prophecies about the unsuspecting visitor. By the time of Jonestown, the staff assignments included gun smuggling, international banking, relations with foreign governments, prostitution and blackmail, torture, and even murder.

The approximately 120-member Planning Commission was Jones's congregation within a congregation. They saw themselves as his board of trustees or church session, selected by him to help make church policy and carry out church discipline. They were, in fact, his guinea pigs, on which he experimented night after endless night. As he wore the Planning Commission into submission, he could in turn use their example to influence the larger congregation. Al Mills explained how it worked when Jones decided the Temple would obey the example of the first-century Christian church and "sell all things and have everything in common" (*see* Acts 4:32).

"There was no high pressure at first; but when one of us on the Planning Commission decided to do it, he made a big example of that person. Gradually, he made it a requirement of Planning Commission members to give all. After he engulfed the Planning Commission into this idea of giving everything to the Temple, he brought the idea to the rest of the church. He told them how the Planning Commission had given all and that they should be doing it too. Then, later on, if anyone would resist, they would be called into counseling."

At first Jones's appointed counselors thought they were there to help people with their prob-

lems. Grace Stoen, who directed the 120 counselors for several years, said, "Though I wasn't
trained to be a counselor—none of us was a
professional—I really tried to help people. We
were on call twenty-four hours a day and some of
us did a lot of good. But more and more I saw
how some counselors were misusing the authority
they had in people's lives." Wayne Pietila remembers the counselors more as policemen and
spies. "Their duty," he told me, "was to make
the people keep the rules and discipline those
who didn't."

Meetings of the staff, the Planning Commission
and the counselors consumed every available
extra hour for only about 250 Temple members.
But the entire church membership was involved
in some dimension of Temple maintenance from
the all-important tasks of collecting monies for
the growing Temple treasuries to keeping the
eleven Greyhound buses in repair, and eventually, clearing a jungle base for the Temple's final
home in Jonestown. Almost everyone, regardless
of his place in the Temple hierarchy of leadership,
worked nonstop for Jones and the People's Temple. Jones demanded it.

Temple Members Lived in a Constant State of Exhaustion

To carry out this wide variety of tasks ranging
from worship to survival training, Jones often
kept Temple members on their feet for twenty-

four hours at a time. Wayne Pietila said, "We would be up all night long, then had to go right to our work or Temple job or school. Then we had to get back to the Temple in time for another all-night meeting. So we were constantly drained." Bonnie Thielmann told us, "We were exhausted all the time. It kept us from having any contact with anybody else at all." Al Mills remembers, "We didn't have time to read anything because we were busy working all the time and too tired to read or talk or even think."

Grace Stoen summarized our subjects' feelings about the state of exhaustion resulting from Jones's abuse of his followers' time. "I was always so tired. I was working eighteen hours every day for the church. One day a week I was working straight through. I'd go home at seven in the morning, take a shower and be back at eight A.M. One time I worked twenty-eight hours straight. So I was really losing sleep. I didn't know what a weekend was for six long years. I felt that I was going to break down. I started fantasizing about going on my hands and knees to Jim Jones asking him, begging him, to let me go to sleep instead of going to another meeting."

Even the children were kept exhausted. Daphene was a child in Redwood Valley. She says of her days in the Temple Junior Choir, "We sat in the balcony for hours. They wouldn't let us out. We would go to sleep, if we could get away with it; but usually somebody would come along and wake us up." Lena Pietila remembers that "even after midnight, when the kids had been there for five or six hours, they wouldn't let them sleep. They were kept up so they could listen. As long as Jones was talking, we all had to listen. But if he started doing his healings, it was okay then to lay the children down." Grace Stoen adds, "It really turned me off that the children, in those long services, had to sleep on the floor until two A.M. Then we had to wake them, put them in the car, freezing cold, and take them home. They never got proper or adequate sleep."

The members of the People's Temple worked day and night. Most of them spent their time doing good. Others of them spent their time doing evil. Regardless of the task each had, Jones made sure his followers were worn out. As a result, they had no time nor energy to read, to contemplate, to interact with other people, to build personal or familial relationships, to gain perspective on the Temple deception, or to do anything about it. They lived more and more in a zombielike state of obedience—too exhausted to care. And though at least temporarily exhilarated by their participation in Jones's utopian dream for them, in the end they were too exhausted to fight back when the dream became a nightmare.

Exhaustion Was a Trap

Jones's defectors remind us to use our time carefully. I have been pastoring a local church for the past three-and-a-half years, and working on church boards and committees for as long as I can remember. Perhaps it is really stretching the point to compare the exhaustion that sets in with workers in our own churches to the exhaustion of Jones's followers. But isn't there a comparison to be made for clergy and laity alike?

Jones's victims were trapped by their own exhaustion. Are we tricked by guilt or pressure techniques (self-imposed or imposed on us by others) into doing jobs we don't want or really need to do? What other worthwhile tasks or opportunities are being sacrificed in the process? What time are we spending on personal renewal, family life, recreation, Bible study, and relaxed, informal discussion? What new books have we read lately? What helpful magazines or journals have we scanned?

What about all our church meetings? Could their number or their length be cut if we managed our time better? Should we limit each other to the one or two church jobs we do well rather than the smattering of jobs we are tempted to accept? Should we require time off or time between jobs for Sunday-school teachers, for board members, for all workers in the church? Should we limit the amount of time church staff and volunteers can work in any one week on church management?

Mrs. Joyce Shaw, a board member of the Human Freedom Center (for six years a member of the Temple), recalls her weariness under

Jones. She participated in a suicide drill, drinking a tiny cup of wine in San Francisco. She knew it wasn't poison, but she was so tired that night, so exhausted from weeks of cat-napping, that she remembers thinking, if it were poison, *It wouldn't be so bad . . . it would be nice . . . so nice, just to go to sleep* (*Los Angeles Times*, December 17, 1978).

For Reflection and Discussion

1. How many hours a week do you spend in worship and "church work"? What part of that time most builds your faith? What part is most destructive of it?

2. Jones quoted Galatians 6:7 to motivate his followers. Considering the way you personally distribute your time, what would you say you are sowing? (Does the question arouse guilt?)

3. What sort of appeals are most effective in getting you to add "just one more thing" to your schedule?

4. Consider God's provision of *rest* for His people. Read Exodus 20:8–11 and Hebrews 4:1–11. How do you use Sunday? What sort of rest do you schedule at other times?

Scripture Text

Galatians 6:7
Do not be deceived; God is not mocked, for whatever a man sows, that he will also reap.

Exodus 20:8–11
"Remember the sabbath day, to keep it holy. Six days you shall labor, and do all your work; but the

seventh day is a sabbath to the Lord your God; in it
you shall not do any work, you, or your son, or your
daughter, your manservant, or your maidservant, or
your cattle, or the sojourner who is within your
gates; for in six days the Lord made heaven and
earth, the sea, and all that is in them, and rested the
seventh day; therefore the Lord blessed the sabbath
day and hallowed it.''

Hebrews 4:1–11

Therefore, while the promise of entering his rest remains, let us fear lest any of you be judged to have
failed to reach it. For good news came to us just as
to them; but the message which they heard did not
benefit them, because it did not meet with faith in
the hearers. For we who have believed enter that
rest, as he has said,

 ''As I swore in my wrath,
 'They shall never enter my rest,' '' although his
works were finished from the foundation of the
world. For he has somewhere spoken of the seventh
day in this way, ''And God rested on the seventh
day from all his works.'' And again in this place he
said,

 ''They shall never enter my rest.''
Since therefore it remains for some to enter it, and
those who formerly received the good news failed to
enter because of disobedience, again he sets a certain day, ''Today,'' saying through David so long
afterward, in the words already quoted,

 ''Today, when you hear his voice,
 do not harden your hearts.''

For if Joshua had given them rest, God would not speak later of another day. So then, there remains a sabbath rest for the people of God; for whoever enters God's rest also ceases from his labors as God did from his. Let us therefore strive to enter that rest, that no one fall by the same sort of disobedience.

5

Jones Kept Them in a State of Poverty and Dependence

The Abuse of Money

Somewhere in Switzerland there may be a bank with millions of dollars of God's money in it. The money was stolen from our brothers and sisters by a man who was building himself a kingdom. He did not take from the rich in order to help the poor; he took from the rich *and* the poor—and mostly the poor—in order to help himself. Jones was a master con man. He bilked his followers out of at least twenty-six million dollars in cash and real estate. He used tired, old tricks we all should recognize by now, tricks *still* being used to steal God's money from His people.

Love Offerings

Jeannie Mills has a collection of Jones's appeal letters that should be mounted in a Christian Hall of Infamy. (*See Appendix* 4.) They give us insights into Jones's skillful use of "special offers" to entice unsuspecting people not already closely associated with the Temple. They weren't just any old gifts, mind you, that were offered. They were "anointed" gifts; and Jones promised that they would bring miracles and blessings to their new owners.

Look in the appendix of this book for samples of Jones's gift list: Three different, full-color, autographed pictures of Pastor Jones were available. Gift number twenty was a container of "anointed oil." Gifts 21–23 were "lovely lockets, each with a picture of Pastor Jones in it." You could also get lockets which Pastor Jones had anointed for protection from evil—untouched by anyone else; and for the children, there were lockets blessed by Pastor Jones especially for their health and safety. If you already had a locket, you could get a key chain blessed for "safety on the road"; a two-minute timer for the meditation which Pastor Jones advised for the safety of all motorists before they went anywhere in a car; or a packet of personalized Temple stationery with a pen and small picture of Pastor Jones.

The list of gifts was endless. Jones had something for everyone's taste. And, as to the cost, the form states: "I also understand that there is no charge for the blessed gift." The gifts were all free. By now we should understand what Jones meant by "free." It would be inconvenient to sell gifts, because then Jones would have to pay taxes and face interstate regulatory agency standards that would threaten his nonprofit corporation status. But, of course, Jones knew that all of Christendom has been conditioned to play that "free gift" game. Christians feel responsible to help pay the cost of producing and mailing what they order. Their offerings were carefully recorded, computed, and averaged, so that the cost of gifts and their mailing could be kept well under the average contribution. Lest anyone make a mistake, Jones did make suggestions as to each item's worth at the bottom of each appeal. He listed places to mark the amount of a "love offering" beginning with five dollars (a minimum suggestion) and going up to one hundred dollars and even "other" (no maximum suggestion is made).

Jones promoted his anointed gifts with testimonials to their effectiveness. Their miracle reports included everything from the cure of A. Guillary's daughter (who had a fever) to the healing of E. Watkins's persimmon tree (which was dying). One testimony by an Eleanor Muldrow reported that her twelve-year-old son went to the hospital with a 103° fever, and after two examinations the doctor diagnosed his illness as meningitis. Mrs. Muldrow wrote that after hearing the doctor's report, "I almost died. That is a horrible crippling, blinding disease. I could not accept this. He was so sick you could almost smell the fever. They tapped his back for spinal fluid and said 'Yes,' it was meningitis, no doubt about it. I was in shock all day and night. Sunday morning I went to the hospital armed with your picture for Child Protection. I rubbed his neck and head with it. He jumped and wanted to know what I had put on him. I told him something cool. He said it wasn't cold, it was hot! . . .

"Well, they did another tap Sunday night . . . but they couldn't find anything. By Wednesday . . . I brought him home. I put your Key Chain Picture in his pocket. . . . Tuesday he went back to school, and today I have a well and happy child.

"This past weekend my offerings were really given from my heart. Sacrifice? Yes, but willing gladly and with thanksgiving and praise. . . . I thank and praise God through you."

Although miracles seemed to be guaranteed, Jones made no promises for the effectiveness of his anointed gifts. On the appeal letter, Jones made sure the people knew ". . . that these blessed gifts work only by faith." There would be no breach-of-promise lawsuits against Jones. He implied a promise of protection and healing for those who gave, and yet it was only the faith of the giver which guaranteed the promise.

Perhaps the worst trick Jones employed in these general appeals to get the money from Temple outsiders was his use of the Bible to support his con game. On the bottom of the mailings were quotes from Scripture. "Jesus said unto him, If thou wilt be perfect, go and sell that thou hast, and give to the poor, and thou shalt have treasure in heaven . . ." (Matthew 19:21 KJV). By now we have established what Jones thought of the Scripture and of Jesus; and yet he used both to deceive and to motivate the outsider. The text made the giver sure the offer was from "a man of God" and tied that man's phony gifts and worthless promises in with Christ's own promises and commands.

Obedience Offerings

Besides the "love offering" Jones used another ploy as a regular method for adding to his growing treasury. For certain contributions Jones offered not gifts but his own personal prayers on the contributor's behalf. A special letter was sent to persons sharing a serious interest in the Temple. In the letter was a prayer cloth and an explanation that Pastor Jim Jones "cares very much for you and meditates often for your problems. He desires that your life be blessed and that your body be free from pain." To receive the greatest blessings from this prayer cloth, it was necessary only to "pin your Prayer Cloth to your clothing today, wear it for two days and two nights, and send it in with your Prayer Sheet which is on the next page." In return for following these instructions, "Pastor Jones will meditate for your needs using your Prayer Sheet and Prayer Cloth for seven days." Simple.

It is a trick as old as Friar Tetzel, who traveled about Germany in the sixteenth century selling

indulgences. "Give a gift and we will release certain spiritual powers on your behalf or on behalf
of those you love." Martin Luther saw through
that trick, and later Roman Catholic reformers
condemned it as well. Now the Protestant entrepreneurs are out-Tetzeling Tetzel. Jones was
neither the first nor the last to offer intercessory
prayer as a "free gift." Turn on your religious
television station. Twenty-four hours a day,
prayer for your needs is offered by at least a
dozen legitimate and illegitimate Christian television personalities and their organizations. There
is no charge, but again, those who offer prayer
know that a needy Christian will sacrifice his last
dollar in hopes that where his prayers have failed,
the prayers of a superstar like Jones may get
through to God.

And Jones never intended that the prayers or
the meditations be free. He called offerings ac-
companying prayer requests his "obedience offering." He wrote "Oh, yes, there is one more
thing: Special blessings come to those who honor
this work of God with their offerings. In recent
meetings there has been a revelation about
OBEDIENCE OFFERINGS of certain amounts.
There are many who have been blessed when
they gave as much as $700.00 or $999.00, and
hundreds of others who received their miracles,
when they gave obediently as they were led by
the Spirit." And how did one know how big an
offering obedience required? Simply "close your

eyes and ask God to show you. When you ask with an honest heart, you will be shown just how much you should give." And (were you tempted to cheat), "God will also reveal to Pastor Jones what your obedience offering should be. It is important that you be honest with God!"

The appeal was not complete without a glossy page of testimonies. In the above instance, the words of praise were framed in rectangular boxes resembling dollar bills, the smiling faces of blessed givers peering out from the spot usually reserved for George Washington. One of these givers, an elderly black woman named Lucille Taylor, wrote: "When my pastor said that $7.77 would cause financial blessings I gave that amount. The very next week I received a check in the mail . . . for $177.00. I believe in miracles because I see them happening every day in my life." Even more miraculous was the experience of Annie Moore: "I had money multiply in a beautiful meeting in People's Temple. During the offering when Pastor Jones asked if anyone had $7.00 I put this amount in. I looked again and $77.00 had miraculously materialized in my wallet. Praise God!" (Annie Moore was one of Jones's staff members and died in Jonestown.)

The Use of Guilt and Fear

Jones's "love offering" and "obedience offering" tricks were nothing in comparison to the Reverend's eventual use of guilt and terror to get money from his flock. Tim Stoen, who before his defection from the Temple in 1977 was Jones's financial advisor, relates a personal example. After many years of service to Jones, working night and day for "the cause" on top of his sixty-hour work week as deputy District Attorney in San Francisco County, Stoen flew to London just to see some Shakespeare. "I was so hungry for culture, I couldn't stand it," explained Stoen, who even bought his clothes at the Salvation Army in obedience to Jones's Spartan demands. "I couldn't even get out of my seat after seeing *Julius Caesar* at the National Theater." Stoen intended to quit the Temple at that point, but Jones begged him to return. When Stoen complied, he was greeted by a grieved and jilted Jim Jones. "How could you do this, Tim?" When the errant disciple tried to explain, Jones replied: "See that tree over there? I don't think anybody in the world has the right to enjoy the fruit off that tree until everybody does."

"And all of a sudden," recalls Stoen, "he hit that old guilt button in me, and I said, 'You're right, you know; I'm being selfish; I'm not denying myself. I'll give it another try.' And that's how he kept me in all this time."

Wayne Pietila, one of Jones's bodyguards, also remembers Jones's use of guilt as a device for bilking followers of their money. Perhaps two thousand people or more would come to the services in San Francisco and Los Angeles, recalls

Pietila. "The kind of services that we held appealed mostly to black or downtrodden people—the oppressed people of the United States. They didn't care about what he said; they heard there was a man there who could heal them of their infirmities."

During these healing services Jones would take a collection, cataloging all the services the Temple was providing for these people: housing and food for the poor and orphaned; medical and legal services; college educations, and so forth. Following this pep talk, the collection was taken—with buckets. Pietila explains that one of his responsibilities was to take the money into a back room, quickly count it, and hand Jones a slip of paper with the recorded amount just received. When Jones thought he could get more than he got in the first collection, "he would say, 'We've only got five hundred dollars,' when in actuality we would have five thousand dollars." Looking back, Pietila adds somberly: "These poor people didn't have anything to give." Yet when they had no more money, "they gave gold rings, diamond rings, watches, Social Security checks, or whatever they had." Wayne remembers getting so many valuables they had to bury them around the Temple in secret caches.

The very reason for the Temple's expansion from Redwood Valley to San Francisco and Los Angeles was apparently the desire for more money, which would lead in turn to increased

power. Jones's aides report that he would frequently say, "If we stay here in the valley, we're
wasted. We could make it to the big time in San
Francisco." He also reportedly said that Los
Angeles "was worth fifteen thousand to twenty-
five thousand dollars a weekend."

But Jones was not even satisfied with the
buckets of money he drew from the hapless victims of his urban healing services. He wanted everything his followers owned. An examination of
real estate records in Los Angeles, San Francisco, and Mendocino Counties shows that the
Temple owned, over the years, over two million
dollars' worth of property. Just how it was ac-
quired in each instance will never be known, because most of the potential witnesses died at
Jonestown. But the story of Wayne and Mabel
Medlock could probably be told many times over.
In a civil suit, they claim to have transferred their
Los Angeles property, valued at $190,000, to the
People's Temple after Jones threatened them
with their lives. "You will sign these papers or
die," they quote Jones as saying.

Usually Jones was more subtle than he was
with the Medlocks. He would more commonly
tell individual followers that he received a revelation to the effect that they would be struck with a
fatal illness or accident, unless they took refuge in
the Ukiah area, giving up all they owned in return
for the Temple's protection and maintenance.
Creditability would be given to such warnings by

announcements in the Temple's newsletter. One TRAGIC NEWS FLASH, for example, reported the strange death of Mrs. Mildred Wallace, a young woman residing in Indianapolis, Indiana. She was instructed by Jim Jones, says the bulletin, to move to Redwood Valley by a certain date. But since she procrastinated and failed to meet the deadline, ". . . she died precisely in the manner that Jim Jones had foreseen and told us all about. She died of a disease which rarely affects a woman as young as she was when she passed."

Persons interested in moving to Ukiah were instructed to talk only with Mrs. Charles Anderson, a real estate broker and member of the Temple. "In some instances," says the newsletter, "she has told people not to buy certain things because they were over their heads financially. If she tells you not to buy, please heed her advice." Naturally, the person instructed not to buy property was encouraged, instead, to live in facilities owned by the Temple. The cost: the total loss of financial autonomy and whatever property the person might happen to own.

Even those who did not live in Temple facilities sacrificed a large portion of their financial independence. Nonresidents of the Temple were expected to give 25 percent of their income. Constant and severe pressures ensured that they did. They were also forbidden to spend their money on new cars, new clothes, movies, eating out, or other such luxuries. And luxuries they already had were subject to seizure. Grace Stoen reports that she once lost her piano to the Temple. "One day they knocked on my door and said, 'We came to get your piano.' Because Jones asked, Grace gave.

Another major source of revenue for the Temple was, at least indirectly, the government. Each month Jones would bus his senior citizens to San Francisco, where the bank would open at 7:00 A.M. to give them their Social Security checks. These checks then went to the Temple, where the elderly members resided. A similar arrangement took place with the emotionally disturbed boys placed in the Temple's charge by the state. Walt Jones and Micki Touchette, both directors of the Temple's "care homes," have stated that most of the eight hundred to one thousand dollars sent monthly to each boy was actually transferred to the Temple. The homes, in turn, were operated on minuscule budgets, made possible by the canned goods and used clothing donated by other Temple members.

Responsible Giving

At the heart of Jones's deception were two ancient ploys. First, Jones promised the people that if they would give, God would reward their giving in extra blessings. We have all heard the expression *You can't outgive God*. And it is true that God's blessings to His people are, in the words of the psalmist, "too wonderful to comprehend."

But we have no guarantee that our giving to God will result in our getting back from God in kind. The widow gave her mite, but it is safe to assume she stayed both poor and a widow after giving it. The Pharisees gave their tithe and remained rich and powerful. To imply to an old woman on welfare that when she gives her entire check to Jones, she will, in turn, receive a gift of money in the mail that more than doubles her sacrifice is a deception. Jesus asked the church to be responsible for the widows among us; and yet the tables have been turned so that widows on small pensions, living in borderline poverty, have become a major source of income to religious entrepreneurs and con men like Jones.

The second ploy Jones practiced was in getting the victims of his financial appeals to believe that they were giving to help others. We have already illustrated the fact that only a small percentage of Jones's final fortune reached the poor and needy. But Jones had mastered the art of the emotional appeal. For a while he promised to provide housing and tuition to college students. Yet the college students we interviewed, who finally defected from Jones, said they were simply crowded into rented rooms and worked day and night for the Temple. The presentation of a "pressing need" is a trick widely used today. Legitimate and illegitimate religious organizations know that people give only to a need that "touches their heart." So those organizations are always in the market for new and more touching needs. But there are ostensibly Christian organizations that rush to the scene of a devastating tragedy, get themselves photographed with victims of that disaster, and feature the "moving" pictures in an appeal letter to those on their mailing list. The appeal notes items of immediate need. A blanket may be listed at ten dollars. The repair of a ruined church may cost one thousand dollars. In *fact*, the blanket may cost two dollars, with eight dollars going to pay the overhead of the man or organization who makes the offer.

Now it is doubly difficult to discriminate between the con man and the saint, because we have forced them both to move us emotionally before we give. And as a result, the real and the phonies among us present bigger and bigger needs and ask us to meet them. We are bombarded by offers to support orphans, new Christian schools and colleges, unreached villages, earthquake victims, starving children, television studios and satellites, retirement homes and full communities, retreat centers and Bible-distribution programs. Some of the needs are real. Some are not. We are left with the responsibility of judging both which needs are legitimate and which legitimate causes are most worth supporting. Some needs must always go unmet.

We must not let Jonestown or the financial deception of so many people by Jones make us skeptical and unwilling to give. People's Temple members believed sincerely that their wealth belonged to "the cause" and not to themselves. They were correct! Our "cause" as Christians is *Christ*, the *Son of God*, and His church at mission in the world. We own nothing. We are only stewards of what has been entrusted to us by God. Here members of the Temple shamed all too many of us by their sacrificial example.

Yet, we must not go on being taken in. We must be *responsible* stewards. We, too, will be victimized, as were those who died in Jonestown, unless we determine at least three things before we give another dollar:

1. Are the advertised needs real and not just another trick for getting us to give?
2. Are those promising to meet the advertised need honest, using our money wisely, and getting the major portion of our money to those who need it? Do they publish a financial statement?
3. Are the advertised needs more significant than the ongoing needs in our local church or in our community, which cannot compete with the media-hyped, overadvertised needs which bombard us?

There is one sad reality. Those who advertise their so-called needs most widely know well that the people most vulnerable to emotional appeal are the old and the poor, who can least afford to

give. Most of us between the ages of fifteen and
fifty-five give very little to outside causes. So
those who give most generously are the ones who
have no way or no energy to find the answers to
the questions I have suggested. They would never
ask the Joneses among us for a financial account-
ing. If they did get a financial statement, it would
be too complex or too deceptive to be understood. They don't check with their pastor or the
Better Business Bureaus to see if the organization
is meeting basic standards of financial responsibility. And they don't have any way to discern
adequately whether the advertised needs are
being met, or just being used to meet someone's
monthly budget.

It seems to me that after Jonestown, we owe it
to these innocent victims—and to ourselves—to
use our local church, our denomination, or a
neutral body to investigate thoroughly all who
advertise needs and make the results of those
studies both simple to understand and available to
all of us. Unless we do something, our people will
go on filling the coffers of con men like Jones,
who will in turn use that money against the kingdom to which it was given.

Jones's coffers were full; it will be years before
the millions are finally accounted for. Why did
Jones hoard the money? What was he planning to
spend it on? Only Jones knew the full answer to
this question—if *he* knew. In all probability, he
did not know specifically how to use the money.

His question to Planning Commission members on how to use the millions was probably sincere. But his ultimate goal he surely knew. Over and over again, former members refer to Jones's obsession with his place in history. He wanted his name to be remembered—alongside the names of Jesus, Lenin, and the Buddha. Even as early as 1965, says Jones's one-time assistant pastor, Ross Case, Jones was instructing his associates to "preach me, and I'll perform miracles to back you up." What *is* clear, then, is that Jim Jones's final goal was the glory of Jim Jones. The means to that end, including the use of Temple funds, were flexible. Community services, strategic contributions, and other uses all played a part.

In recent weeks, the *other uses* have become a major source of intrigue. Without a doubt, the most dramatic possible use of Temple resources was the funding of an alleged death squad. And if one of Jones's top aides and mistresses in recent years, is to be believed, Jones planned to use the $3 million cash found at Jonestown to pay for contracts on his enemies. Thus, to ensure that his name would live on, it appears that Jones was willing to finance—even from his grave—the death of his enemies.

For Reflection and Discussion

1. How much of your money do you give to the church? How do you deal with Malachi 3:8–10? with Matthew 19:21?
2. Consider your church's "stewardship campaigns," if it conducts them. Is "stewardship Sunday" a prime time for a trip to the beach? Why?
3. What motivates you to give to your church? to "causes" outside the church?
4. To what causes outside the church do you actually contribute? How have you (or will you!) verify their legitimacy?
5. In the "Parable of Sower," Matthew 13:22 says that delight in (RSV) or the deceitfulness of (KJV) riches "chokes the word." Consider with respect to Jones. Consider with respect to yourself. Consider with respect to your church.

Scripture Text

Malachi 3:8–10

"Will man rob God? Yet you are robbing me. But you say, 'How are we robbing thee?' In your tithes and offerings. You are cursed with a curse, for you are robbing me; the whole nation of you. Bring the full tithes into the storehouse, that there may be food in my house; and thereby put me to the test, says the Lord of hosts, if I will not open the windows of heaven for you and pour down for you an overflowing blessing."

Matthew 19:21
Jesus said to him, "If you would be perfect, go, sell what you possess and give to the poor, and you will have treasure in heaven; and come, follow me."

Matthew 13:22
"As for what was sown among thorns, this is he who hears the word, but the cares of the world and the delight in riches choke the word, and it proves unfruitful."

Jim Jones, at age ten, poses for family album photo with two cousins in Lynn, Indiana. He became a Christian when a child. (Wide World Photo) *Below:* The house on Regent Street in Berkeley, California, where the Human Freedom Center is located, as a place of refuge for cult defectors and members of Concerned Relatives.

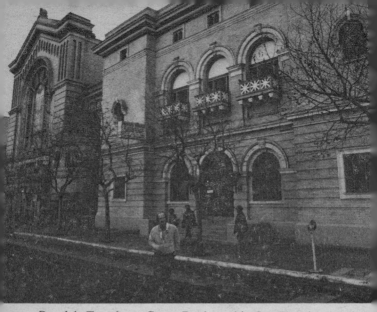

People's Temple on Geary Boulevard in San Francisco. *Below*, Grace and Tim Stoen, both important Temple leaders before their defection, hold a picture of their little family. Their son, John Victor, was held by Jones.

This snapshot of Jones with some of the children in his congregation underscores the multiracial nature of his ministry. *Below:* Daphene Mills joined the Temple with her parents when she was a child.

Bonnie Thielmann, a Temple member for six years, was the daughter of missionaries and attended a Christian college. *Below:* Jim Jones and his wife, Marcie, a nurse. Bonnie lived with them in Brazil.

A typical picture of the "Father" at the mike. Jones, wearing sunglasses, talked endlessly.

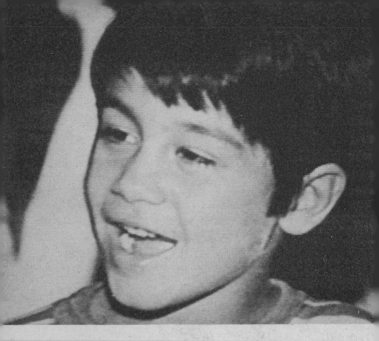

John Victor Stoen, who died at Jonestown, his body next to Jones. *Below:* Sherwin Harris, a Concerned Relative, who went to Guyana with Congressman Ryan's party. He lost his wife and daughters—their throats were slashed in Georgetown.

Jean Mills, a former member of the Temple's important Planning Commission, talks to author Mel White about the cult in the kitchen on Regent Street. *Below:* Al Mills, a social activist of the sixties, who joined the Temple because Jones was helping the poor and oppressed.

Wayne and Lena Pietila with their child. Wayne joined the con
gregation as a teenager and was a personal bodyguard fo
"Father." *Below:* Author interviews Clare Bouquet at th
Hyatt Regency Hotel. Her son, Bryan, died at Jonestown.

6

Jones Kept Them in a State of Fear

The Abuse of Discipline

I sat at the long oak table in the house on Regent Street, drinking too much coffee and listening to too many horror stories from the defectors who had lived them. The secret world of the cults is a world of psychological and physical cruelty. If I needed proof, I could see spread on the table the colored pictures of the heaps of bodies at Jonestown. I could not take it all in, and Jeannie Mills must have seen my wide eyes and open mouth.

She said to me, "I don't expect you to understand. A person who has never experienced a cult is simply not equipped to understand how or why people can allow themselves and others to be abused by another person. But a guy was here yesterday who said, 'Hey, I was in a cult for seven years. I got beat. I almost lost my vision.' He understood. But that's what it takes to understand. You can't intellectually understand what I'm saying." I had to agree.

But there are many who do understand. Jeannie repeated that unbelievable statistic from NBC Television. "There are eight million people in the United States right now who are doing the same thing, and who would die or kill for their leader." She said, "It's not just one individual that you don't understand: millions of people are in the same position as those who took the poison in Jonestown. They're scared. They feel guilty. They don't know which way to go. And they've got one man they feel they can trust." A part of that trust is a willingness to suffer punishment at the hands of the leader.

Types of Punishment

Several types of punishment were used by Jones, their harshness increasing over the course of time. At first, punishment was limited to verbal humiliation.

Temple members, especially the staff, would join with Jones in punishing a person verbally by screaming accusations until the victim cried or tried to run from the room.

The periods devoted to such activities were called "catharsis sessions." The Greek word *catharsis* means to purge or cleanse. The idea was that members of the church would share their weaknesses with one another and receive "instruction" from the group, both verbally and physically. "Usually," recalls Jeannie Mills, "you didn't have to confess—there was someone who turned you in first."

For Jones verbal abuse in the confession or catharsis sessions soon seemed inadequate. It was not long before he added mild whippings to his repertoire of reinforcements. Says Jeannie Mills, "I was whipped for drinking a glass of wine—three hits with a belt." (Wine was one of those luxuries forbidden to members of the Temple—at least until such time as everyone in the world could enjoy it.) As a new member, says Jeannie, she was unaware that wine was forbidden, and someone told on her.

She did not like the fact that she was whipped for the infraction: "It made me mad; it was insulting; it was humiliating . . . . But half the church had had it too. Besides, I hadn't been hit since I was six years old, so maybe I needed it." And so the process of rationalization would go.

The whippings got more and more severe, and the victims more in number. The Mills's fifteen-year-old daughter Linda was once struck seventy-five times on the bottom with a board, euphemistically known as the "board of education." Her friends at school, who saw her when she dressed down for gym class, said that "she looked like hamburger." And what was the sin which warranted such an excruciating "education"? She was seen in the church parking lot, simply hugging a friend she had not seen for some time.

The justification given for the punishment was

that Linda's friend was a lesbian; but the real
reason for the punishment was that Linda was
associating with someone who had left the
church. Even this assault, which kept their
daughter from sitting down for a week and a half,
could be rationalized. Jones must be doing the
right thing, they reasoned; otherwise, why would
so many people keep saying, "Thank you,
Father. I guess I needed that."

Jones's collection of physical punishments
showed more imagination than just beatings. One
of his favorites was boxing matches. But he never
set them up so that there was really a match. He
would always arrange for two unequal opponents,
say, an old man and a healthy teenager. Or
perhaps a man and a woman. Perched securely in
his ringside seat, he would watch with glee as the
"guilty" party received blows from his (or her)
superior opponent. Often a person would be
knocked unconscious.

Still another punishment, applied with relish by
"Father": snakes were held close to the body of
those who were afraid of them. These were not
poisonous snakes, but they did not need to be for
those who feared them sufficiently. Screams from
the individual being punished meant nothing—
beyond the fact that the chosen instrument of
wrath was working to Jones's perverted satisfaction.

There were other types of punishment in addi-
tion to the purely physical that were frequently

employed. These would be tailored to the individual's temperament and psychological makeup. Ross Case mentioned one dear old lady, known for her saintliness and dignity, who was forced upon occasion to use dirty words in public. He identified her as an eighty-year-old Christian, loved for her sweetness and old-fashioned manners. She would reportedly come home from a worship service—to use the term loosely—and announce with great sadness that Pastor Jones made her cuss again.

Probably the most devastating of all punishments, though, was rejection by one's friends and family—a punishment Jones could induce because of his power over Temple members. This would produce psychological wounds which, unlike even the harshest of beatings, might never heal.

Wayne Pietila vividly remembers the time he was "on the hot plate," allegedly for going to bed with a young lady he had been dating. Wayne says that the charge was untrue, but that did not matter. In People's Temple, the accused individual was automatically guilty—without even the option of proving himself innocent. Wayne recalls walking into a meeting of the Planning Commission, of which he was a member, and being greeted by a wall of reproachful stares. After a few points of business were taken care of, Wayne's name was brought up for discussion. When the fallacious charge was voiced, "Jones

looked at me and said, 'Son, where have I failed?'
He was trying to lay a heavy trip on me.'' But that
was insignificant compared to the next three
hours.

"At that time there were probably thirty people
on the Planning Commission, and everybody had
a chance to chew on me and question me, and I
had to answer everything.'' Throughout the entire ordeal, the accused party had to stand—
"sweating and feeling like an ass.'' After
everyone had been given the opportunity to be-
rate the latest delinquent, other business would
be dealt with for an hour or so, but the person had
to remain standing while everyone else was
seated on the floor. Finally, Jones would come
back to the defendant and pronounce judgment. If
the collective reproach of the community was not
deemed sufficient punishment, a whipping might
be thrown in for good measure.

Grace Stoen underwent a similar punishment;
but in her case her husband's scorn was added to
the group's. On this particular occasion, there
was not even an infraction. She was punished
simply because she had not been broken to
Jones's satisfaction. She recalls that one night
after the Planning Commission was adjourned, an
ad hoc meeting was held to which persons sym-
pathetic to Grace were excluded. Before entering
the meeting, she asked if it was about her. Despite assurance that it was not, she soon discovered that it was *only* about her. The ten or twelve

persons present asked if she loved Tim, her husband. When she responded in the affirmative, they began screaming at her, calling her foul names. And when she looked at Tim for reassurance, he denied that he loved her and said that he was married to the cause.

Says Grace, reflecting on that meeting, "It's a miracle that I didn't go home and commit suicide." Despite her independence, she confesses to having always been an insecure person, a person with feelings of inferiority, and a person who cried at the drop of a hat. "And here Tim . . . it just crushed me."

Years later she was told that Tim was very much in love with her, and would even have followed her out of the Temple had she decided to leave. That is precisely why Jones had his loyal aides try to break her in this miserable way. Ironically, the way Jones persuaded Tim Stoen to go along with the plan was by saying that Grace had to be made strong. "People must learn to follow principles and not rely on spouses for emotional support," he would say.

Reasons for Punishment

Making people strong for the sake of the cause was always Jones's means of justifying the cruelties he imposed upon his followers. When Wayne Pietila joined the Temple in the mid-sixties, people had to become strong for the coming nuclear holocaust. Wayne remembers Jones's using this explanation in an incident involving Wayne's two and a half-year-old brother. The entire church, which had only about 150 members at the time, was camping in Oregon. Many rugged moments were endured by the members of this expedition, ostensibly so that they would be toughened up for the holocaust. Three of those rugged moments occurred each day with some regularity: the meals they had to eat. This was not an insurmountable problem for most of the campers: but for little Tommy—admittedly somewhat spoiled in Wayne's estimation—this was sometimes a bit much. Jones, in his desire to see that everyone was strong enough for the dire events he predicted, was determined to eradicate any misbehavior, however young the perpetrator. For Tommy this meant eating the food prepared for that occasion, whatever his notions of good taste. When he screamed and refused to eat, Jones spoon-fed him. And when he proceeded to throw up what he ate, "Jones spooned his vomit back into his mouth." Not once, but three times—until at last, the boy kept it down. With a smile of satisfaction, Jones announced that Tommy would now be able to hide in the bush without crying, should the enemy advance on the remnant from Redwood Valley.

Remember that Jones's prophesy of doom receded as our national fear of nuclear destruction faded in favor of other concerns through the sixties. In the place of Jones's apocalyptic vision came his dreams for the formation of a utopian community. For years, beginning in about 1970, Jones would talk about this new life that he and his blessed followers were going to enjoy. He was not talking about Guyana at first. The exact location was unknown. Perhaps Africa. Perhaps Chile (before the overthrow of Allende). Perhaps Peru. But wherever the place, it was going to be a community the likes of which had never been seen—a model for the world. But for such a vision to become a reality, the people had to be prepared. A perfect community (however defined) would require perfect inhabitants. Thus Jones would say to the members of his Planning Commission, as Jeannie Mills remembers, "Certain people in the congregation require discipline in order to make this a strong group."

I felt both shock and disgust as each defector finished his or her contribution to Jones's growing list of cruelties in the name of making the community strong. Jones was a sadist of the first order and his treatment of others was nothing short of barbaric. But if this is our only response to Jones's use of confession and discipline, we have learned little and turned the event into a cheap source of entertainment—rather like a third-rate horror film.

Although Jones's followers told me they hated the verbal and physical cruelty sometimes meted out at catharsis meetings at the Temple, most of them agreed that there was also benefit in having a place where they could share their sins and receive forgiveness and discipline from the community. An amazing number of defectors even told me that the discipline they received in the Temple was a turning point in their lives, causing them "to go in the right direction."

As they talked about the role of confession and discipline in People's Temple, I couldn't help but think that as Jones erred in his excess, we Christians err in our neglect of both confession and discipline in our churches. Most Christians are encouraged to confess sinfulness (usually in the vaguest sense) at conversion, but there is no provision for regular, systematic confession of the specific sins committed after conversion.

And there is almost no chance in most churches to receive forgiveness and discipline by Christian peers. Occasionally a divorcee or adulterer is shamed by a group of church fathers, or someone is asked to give up teaching or leading "for a while," but church discipline is not generally practiced among us with any degree of consistency or concern. Have we sidestepped and soft-pedaled the role of the Christian community in disciplining the believer because we are too kindly—or too cowardly?

We look at Jones's practices with a sense of anger and unbelief. But again, despite or even partly because of them, Temple members remember Jones with a strange mixture of hatred and fondness. And no doubt the ready reacceptance of an offender by the community was a key factor. When Jones got particularly abusive he would often make amends with the person later. In an interview with *New West* magazine, Al Mills reenacts Jones's typical approach to the humiliated disciple: "Jim would come over and put his arms around the person and say, 'I realize that you went through a lot, but it was for the cause. Father loves you and you're a stronger person now. I can trust you more now that you've gone through this and accepted this discipline!' " And it was accepted.

After leaving our churches, those who went to Jones seemed relieved to find a community which cared enough about them to take their problems and weaknesses seriously—and yet not to reject them permanently. And though each has suffered from Jones's psychological and physical violence, I am convinced that because of his apparent concern for them, and because of the close community he created for a time, they may find our Christian communities to be strangely dishonest and disinterested by comparison.

For Reflection and Discussion

1. Read 1 John 1:8 and James 5:16. Ponder/discuss whether you think our communities' tendency to ignore sins or sweep them under the rug encourages self-deception and/or leaves us carrying a great burden of guilt.

2. Dietrich Bonhoeffer wrote in *Life Together:*

   "In confession the breakthrough to community takes place. Sin demands to have a man by himself. It withdraws him from the community. The more isolated a person is, the more destructive will be the power of sin over him, the more deeply he becomes involved in sin, the more disastrous the isolation."

   What are your reactions to this statement?

3. What sort of discipline, if any, does your church practice? Who would be most likely to be censured, and under what circumstances?

4. Scripture makes a number of comments on discipline; among them are 1 Corinthians 5:11, 2 Corinthians 7:8–10, and Galatians 6:1. Read these passages. What do you consider to be the characteristics of constructive discipline?

Scripture Text

1 John 1:8
If we say we have no sin, we deceive ourselves, and the truth is not in us.

James 5:16
Therefore confess your sins to one another, and pray for one another, that you may be healed. The prayer of a righteous man has great power in its effects.

1 Corinthians 5:11
But rather I wrote to you not to associate with any

one who bears the name of brother if he is guilty of immorality or greed, or is an idolater, reviler, drunkard, or robber—not even to eat with such a one.

2 Corinthians 7:8–10
For even if I made you sorry with my letter, I do not regret it (though I did regret it), for I see that that letter grieved you, though only for a while. As it is, I rejoice, not because you were grieved, but because you were grieved into repenting; for you felt a godly grief, so that you suffered no loss through us. For godly grief produces a repentance that leads to salvation and brings no regret, but worldly grief produces death.

Galatians 6:1
Brethren, if a man is overtaken in any trespass, you who are spiritual should restore him in a spirit of gentleness. Look to yourself, lest you too be tempted.

7

Jones Kept Them in a State of Sexual Bondage

The Abuse of Sexuality

Time, Newsweek, and all the "instant books" on Jonestown have featured explicit accounts of the deviant sexual practices of the madman Jones. I must admit that I, too, have been surprised and embarrassed by the stories my subjects have told me from their own experience about Jones's apparent preoccupation with sex. It seemed to dominate his personal life and public pronouncements.

But to dismiss Jones's sexual practices as simply a sign of his moral sickness is to miss the complex and powerful force sex has been in the forming and maintaining of cults through the ages. And to shake our heads in disbelief that our brothers and sisters could fall for his sexual lies so easily is to forget two underlying realities. First, Jones was a master at making his lies very close to being truth; and, second, once persons had committed themselves to his greater lie about the brave new world they were building, they were terribly vulnerable to any lesser lies he told along the way.

The Sacrifice of Sexual Standards for the Cause

Although the press has revealed the lurid details of Jones's most recent sexual behaviors, we must remember his use of sex to dominate and control his followers began much more subtly. Bonnie Thielmann, a temple defector, says her exposure to Jones's sexual views was when she lived with Jim and Marcie in Brazil in 1961. Bonnie was seventeen. The Joneses lived in an apartment overlooking Copacabana Beach. "One day," Bonnie told us, "Jones made a big thing about how he sold himself to a Brazilian diplomat's wife for five thousand dollars to feed hungry children."

Bonnie remembers clearly how she felt when she heard that Jones had spent three days in bed with a Brazilian woman in order to aid the poor. She said, "Most people hearing that would go, 'Yuck,' but when I found out about it, I thought, 'Here I am with my little puritanical moral code about my body and my virginity and there is a couple [Jim and Marcie] who care so much that they were willing to put much worse than their lives on the line. They were willing to sell their bodies.' That act," she confessed, "only added to the fact that I was impressed by their caring, their loving, their compassion. Now, however," she added, "I realize I don't even know if the story was true or not. I mean, it could be a total lie.''

It probably was a lie. Jones loved a good story, especially one that would serve his manipulative purposes. Whether the story was fact or fiction, in one Brazilian "parable" Jones had set up the tension for a young girl that, a decade later, would end in what she confesses was "a total loss of any basis for morality." He set one truth up against another. Which is more important: to maintain technical virginity or to feed a starving child?

Jones forced an attractive and impressionable young woman, the daughter of missionaries, to choose between the Seventh Commandment, "Thou shalt not commit adultery," and Christ's clear command to feed the poor and care for the orphans. It may simply have been Jones's way of seducing a pretty young girl, but for her, the choice created a major ethical crisis.

In a sermon ten years later, Jones created a similar crisis for the same young woman. Bonnie heard Jones say to the congregation in Redwood Valley, "You people are so selfish. You go to bed with a good-looking person, but what about these old black people who have never had sex? They have never had anyone to love them. If you really cared, if you really loved people, you would be willing to go to bed with some old black person that didn't look so good to you."

She remembers approaching Jones in the parking lot after the service. "I had picked out an obnoxious old man in the church," she remembers. "He was eighty-seven years old. He talked on and on and on. There was nothing attractive about him. But I knew he was lonely. So I told Jones I would go to bed with the old man. Jones put his hand on my shoulder and said, 'That's sweet.' That is all he said."

Jones constructed a most difficult moral dilemma. And before we rush to judge the decisions his followers made along the way, we need to ask ourselves how adequately prepared we have been to decide any differently. They were building a community that would save the world. They were running out of time. They were exhausted, isolated, frightened, and confused. Jones asked them to sacrifice their sexual standards for the cause. Under such difficult circumstances—or even in the face of the pressures of daily life— how *do* we come to decisions?

It is one thing to teach that the Bible is "inerrant" or "fully authoritative and trustworthy." It is something else to understand the Bible well enough for it to guide us through the difficult decisions we must make every day. Let's let Jonestown goad us into new frankness in our Bible studies. Let's let Jonestown get us into an honest discussion in our churches of the difficult choices we must make. And, above all, let's let Jonestown keep us from being arrogant and judgmental when others who are isolated and under pressure make the wrong decisions.

The Sacrifice of Sexual Acts for the Cause

In 1978 Jones cracked down even harder on his flock. That year, Wayne Pietila remembers, Jones finally made it official: "There will be no sex for anyone in the Temple," Jones said. Some defected immediately after this mandate. But most people stayed and went along with it, even the married couples who followed Jones. Let's examine the reasons it seemed so logical to give up sex entirely for the cause.

Wayne and Lena can think of at least two reasons that Jones imposed sexual abstinence on his followers. First, it was a discipline. "You know, if you could abstain from sex, it made you a better, stronger person. It proved you could control yourself." And, second, Wayne recalls, "Jones was thinking, if people were getting together to have sex and the married couples were moving back together at home, they wouldn't be paying much attention to what he was teaching them. And so he would lose control of the whole family situation."

From the beginning of "communities" in America, celibacy or sexual abstinence has been a central tenet in maintaining commitment to the community. Jones was preparing his people to survive in the wilderness. It was easy for him to convince most of his followers—at least in principle— that to abstain from sexual intercourse—at least temporarily—was not that great a sacrifice in light of the community's ultimate goals. Not only did his strategy fit three hundred years of community history in America, but it fit the Pauline New Testament pattern as well. Deep within the Christian backgrounds of Jones's followers were at least memories of the Apostle Paul's saying, in light of Christ's imminent return, ". . . The time we live in will not last long. While it lasts, married men should be as if they had no wives . . ." (1 Corinthians 7:29 NEW ENGLISH BIBLE).

Because of the urgency and importance of the cause, Jones asked people to sacrifice sexual intercourse. To people already working twenty-four hours a day, he said that their sacrifice would save time for the cause. To people already exhausted, he said that their sacrifice would save them energy. To people anxious to please, he gave one more opportunity to prove their love and loyalty.

But there were other less altruistic reasons to impose abstinence, and Jones must have known them well. When couples spend time together making love, intimacy is created that threatens total commitment to the community. There is time to talk, to compare notes, to share doubts, to give each other strength to resist and support to fight back. Al and Jeannie Mills told me they made a simple commitment to each other when they joined the People's Temple. "No matter what happens," they promised each other, "we will not stop talking and we will not stop making love." It wouldn't hurt any of us who work in the church to remember their simple commitment. It saved their marriage, their lives, and the lives of their family. Others weren't so fortunate.

For the greater good, married couples moved into bunk beds, and from bunk beds to separate dormitories, and from separate dorms to assignments in distant cities. The destructive side of sexual sacrifice became immediately apparent. Most of the Temple marriages were left in shambles, and with the opportunity for normal sexual relationships discontinued, Jones moved into an even more bizarre stage in the sexual history of People's Temple.

Jones Substituted Himself in Their Sexual Fantasies

We don't know exactly what pushed Jones to this next stage. Did his narcissism and sexual fantasies drive him completely mad, or was he a clever, thorough diabolical strategist keeping one step ahead of his congregation's sexual needs? Whatever happened, sex began to dominate much of Jones's Temple tirades.

Jones listed himself on the Temple's organizational chart as "the Main Body." He took the self-given compliment quite literally and bragged about his physical size and prowess in public and in private.

Jones was consciously building a sexual image

he hoped his people would focus on in their own fantasies. I am guessing it was because he couldn't afford to have people daydreaming about relationships with others in the Temple. He needed their total attention and their total loyalty. So he needed to substitute himself—even in their sexual fantasies.

He insisted posters of movie stars or sports figures come down and be replaced by posters of Jim Jones. Lena Pietila, a teenager at the time, commented, "Jones, in public meetings—even before the children—would go on a tangent about his sexual abilities, describing how all women wanted him and men wanted him as well." Sandy Rozynko Mills was only fourteen when she received a questionnaire from Jones, addressed to the youth of the Temple, asking, "Do you fantasize about Father sexually?" She said, "Here I was, fourteen years old, and I was thinking '*What . . .?*' But we all knew we were supposed to answer *yes*, so I said *yes*."

Whether Jones succeeded in establishing himself as the sex symbol in the fantasies of his congregation is difficult to determine. He went so far as to insist on their signing confessions that he had in fact succeeded. Jeannie Mills had to sign a confession that she had begged Jones to have sex with her, when actually she and her husband were secretly maintaining sexual relations by getting themselves appointed as the codirectors of a Temple rest home where they lived together.

Jones Substituted Himself as Their Sex Partner

It was a natural next step for the Temple's "Main Body" to force himself sexually upon those who might refuse. Wayne Pietila narrates the time it almost happened to him.

"For about three months I had a slight love affair with a young girl. I was nineteen and she was about fifteen. There wasn't any sexual intercourse involved. We just dated. We kissed and she felt really guilty about it and sent a note confessing it to Jones. So, the next Planning Commission meeting I attended, everyone was staring at me." The kangaroo-court type trial that followed has been described in chapter six. Three hours of confrontation by Jones and his Planning Commission were concluded by Jones's verdict: "Wayne, you and I will have to spend more time together." "What he meant was he was going to take me to bed. And I answered, 'No thanks, Father, I don't need that kind of contact from you.'"

Jones couldn't stand the idea of intimacy inside the Temple with anyone but himself. He used his sexual powers both to keep people loyal to himself and to keep people from building relationships with one another that might lead to his eventual undoing.

From many widely publicized reports on Jones's alleged sex activities most of us have turned away in disgust. "The man was crazy," some of us explain it. "The man was demon-possessed," others suggest. And who could deny that Jones was both crazy and demonic; but merely labeling him may cause us to miss the moral of this story. After all, his sexual craziness accomplished exactly what he wanted. His sexual "demons" helped him dominate the people more effectively than any other of his evil schemes.

Obviously, sex is an incredible force in every area of our lives. Our sexuality has potential for great good or for great evil. Once my sexuality is set loose on the course of evil, the rest of me runs, puffing and frantic, in the same direction. No wonder sex has always permeated the rites of the occult. Occultists know what a key factor it is in the organization of our whole personality. Sexual inroads go far and deep.

David, the second great Hebrew king, learned the hard way that after giving in to sexual evil, it is only a short distance to giving in to lies and murder as well. Samson, the giant Hebrew judge, learned the hard way that once we are vulnerable to another person sexually, that person gains power over every other area of our lives. Sexual vulnerability within the context of mutual trust and lifelong commitment can lead to growth for both people; but outside that context—as painfully learned by Samson and the followers of Jim Jones—giving yourself sexually to another person may lead to death.

134 *Deceived*

Jones Used His Sexual Power Against Them

Jones also used sex to dominate, blackmail, punish, and control. Even the children were not immune. Daphene Mills was only ten when she learned from her playmates that Jones was having sex with the little boys "to punish them."

Jones and his henchwomen developed sexual blackmail into an art form. It began innocently enough. The Planning Commission members were asked to sign confessions that he could use against them "for the cause," if ever they decided "against the greater community good." Jeannie Mills told me, "Jones was preparing his defense against traitors; and since we knew then that we would never leave, we signed his 'confessions' gladly. We wrote that we had sex with our children, that we had begged Jones to have sex with us, and that he consented and was fantastic, and all kinds of other weird, bizarre things that nobody really wanted coming back at them. In fact, every time we went to a service, he had us sign a blank piece of paper that he could then fill out with any confession about us he invented."

Slowly he gained sexual domination over their lives, sometimes with their help, as in the trumped-up confessions described above. Other times he worked deviously and deceptively in the dark.

One of my subjects, whose confidentiality I must guard, told me of her own personal experience of Jones's sexual blackmail techniques.

"Jones got one of his top aides to seduce me. They supposedly hid a tape recorder in our room and gave Jones the tape. One morning at 3:00 A.M., one of Jones's staff persons, Carolyn Layton, called me and said, 'We just received a terrible tape recording and you are on it. We're sending a car for you immediately.' They knew I had been resisting Jones's teachings. They had already broken up my marriage. I had lost my belief in anything or anybody. I was ready to quit. So they set up this affair.

"One of Jim's bodyguards had been really nice to me. He sat down beside me and asked how I was doing. We began to talk a little. What I didn't know was that he was seeing me with the permission of the Temple.

"So in the middle of the night they came. They took my child away from me and drove me to the church. A whole catharsis group was waiting. Jim Jones was there, too, and he said to me, 'For God's sake, don't tell Marcie; this would kill her.'

"I knew his wife would have known the whole thing was a setup. Anyway, they told me they had a terrible tape of me having sex with another man. And I asked to hear the tape. Layton answered, 'Oh, it would be too humiliating for you to hear it, you know. We wouldn't ask that of you.'

"I never heard the tape; and it wasn't long after that I managed to escape the Temple. What they wanted was to get somebody intimate with me to find out where I was psychologically. Then they would blackmail me. They blackmailed ninety percent of the congregation."

Jones used sex to gain and maintain power over the lives of people in the Temple, but he also used sex to gain and maintain power over the lives of people outside the Temple. There is little doubt that many such persons were compromised. Undoubtedly in the days ahead, individual confessions will surface. Reputations will be ruined. The final body count may go on.

For Reflection and Discussion

1. What other power has a person with whom you have been in love and/or sexually intimate had over you?
2. Traditionally, the church has considered sexual sins to be among the most serious, and has censured them very severely. Do you agree with that judgment? Why or why not?
3. How do you deal with conflicts in the sexual area? Is there openness to talk about such matters in your church or fellowship group?
4. The Bible comments on our proneness to be corrupted "through deceitful lusts" (Ephesians 4:22). Consider your own needs and behavior, the actions of Jones, and the actions of Jones's followers in the light of such Scriptures as these: Genesis 2:22–25; 1 Corinthians 7:1–5; 1 Corinthians 6:9; Ephesians 5:5–7.

Scripture Texts

Genesis 2:22–25
And the rib which the Lord God had taken from the man he made into a woman and brought her to the man. Then the man said, 'This at last is bone of my bones and flesh of my flesh; she shall be called Woman, because she was taken out of Man.' Therefore a man leaves his father and his mother and cleaves to his wife, and they become one flesh. And the man and his wife were both naked, and were not ashamed.

1 Corinthians 7:1–5
Now concerning the matters about which you wrote. It is well for a man not to touch a woman. But because of the temptation to immorality, each man should have his own wife and each woman her own husband. The husband should give to his wife her conjugal rights, and likewise the wife to her husband. For the wife does not rule over her own body, but the husband does; likewise the husband does not rule over his own body, but the wife does. Do not refuse one another except perhaps by agreement for a season, that you may devote yourselves to prayer; but then come together again, lest Satan tempt you through lack of self-control.

1 Corinthians 6:9
. . . Do not be deceived; neither the immoral, nor idolaters, nor adulterers . . . will inherit the kingdom of God.

Ephesians 5:5–7
Be sure of this, that no fornicator or impure man, or
one who is covetous (that is, an idolater), has any
inheritance in the kingdom of Christ and of God. Let
no one deceive you with empty words, for it is because of these things that the wrath of God comes
upon the sons of disobedience.

8

Jones Kept Them in a State of Isolation

The Abuse of Intimacy

Do you remember those first pictures sent back from Jonestown by Don Harris and his NBC crew before they were murdered? The videotapes record a group working together, playing together, and eating together, in apparent brotherhood and harmony. Even Congressman Ryan was taken in at first by this seemingly loving community. Then, suddenly, a Jonestown resident thrust a note into Harris's hand. "Four of us want to leave," it said. Other cultists were secretly signaling Ryan's party that they too wanted to defect. When Ryan asked Jones if the defectors could go with him, Jones answered, "Anyone is free to come and go. I want to hug them before they leave." Seconds later his mood changed completely and Jones added bitterly, "They will try to destroy us. They always lie when they leave."

Even as Jones's world crumbled around him, he tried to maintain the illusion of intimacy with his followers. But Jones's embrace was not an act

of love, but of bondage. He had to hold them
loyal to himself with his feigned love for them—or
they would destroy him. On the surface, they
were a happy, loving community. But beneath the
surface his demands on theirrelationship kept
them cut off from the outside world and from each
other. He allowed them no other source of intimacy than his own, and then used that relationship to destroy them. Every defector from the
Temple I interviewed shared the sentiments of
Bonnie Thielmann, who described her time with
the People's Temple. "I was totally isolated,"
she said. Every one of Jones's techniques contributed to the isolation of his people. And in significant ways, it was this tragic state of isolation
that eventually resulted in their deaths.

Temporal Isolation

Every person associated with the Temple was
subjected to a rigorous schedule. We have discussed Jones's abuse of his followers' time in
chapter 4; but it is important to establish clearly
the reason he kept the people exhausted. He told
them they were working to create a better world.
He told them the long days and endless nights
were spent to build a community of love and justice and peace. But in fact a primary reason that
he kept them exhausted was to keep them isolated from others, both outside and inside the
Temple.

Wayne Pietila told me that "[membership in]

the People's Temple was a full-time job. You're cut off from every person you've known throughout your life." This was even true for elementary-school children. Daphene Mills, who was only seven when her family joined the Temple, remembers "staying up all hours of the night listening to Jim Jones." One brochure sent out to Temple members outlined a new program for children, which included "sports, tutoring, swimming instruction, and special classes teaching foreign languages, homemaking, first aid and other important subjects."

The brochure goes on to say that the children would be divided by age groups. "Each group chooses the type of activities it wants to participate in throughout the quarter, and then they meet throughout the week for classes and tutoring." To counter the criticism which might follow from making such time demands, the brochure explains: "Although this seems like a busy schedule for these children, the amazing thing is that their grades in public school actually improve, and so does their general health, as they participate in this program." The idea behind the program was clearly to protect the children from the influence of outsiders. In fact, Daphene says she was even taught that "you couldn't play with people who were outside the group."

Picture them in Redwood Valley or San Francisco or in the jungle working from sunrise till sunset. They thought they were building a city.

Instead, they were busy digging their own graves. And by the end of the day they were too tired even to consider posing the questions that might have freed them. The abuse of time leads to exhaustion—leads to being more easily deceived. It is a sequence that holds true in all the cults. Those young men and women selling books and magazines on the street or in the airport concourse usually have quotas to meet before the day can end. Their masters, like Jones, know that it is absolutely necessary to keep them busy. That way they will be too tired to think, too tired to doubt, too tired to read or argue or build relationships, and finally, too tired to escape.

Intellectual Isolation

As Jones insulated his followers from the world at large through the monopoly of their time and the exhaustion that followed, he simultaneously set out to control their minds. Remember, from the beginning he took away the Bible, forbidding them even to carry it to worship. He took away the newspapers, or warned them not to read them. Then, he himself read from the newspapers in their services, explaining and interpreting them as a means of further control. He had a library of ten thousand volumes in Jonestown, but he decided which books would be in it and who could read them. In all my interviews with the defectors, they could remember only one book that Jones insisted they read. It was an introduction to socialism by an author everyone has forgotten.

Jones took away their access to most films and plays, as well. He had good reason to mistrust great and thoughtful drama. Remember, Tim Stoen, having just seen *Julius Caesar* in London, sat transfixed by the ideas that came to him while watching the play. Soon afterward Stoen defected. Occasionally Jones would recommend a film. Once, doing so got him into trouble. Wayne Pietila remembers the time Jones recommended that everyone see the film *Marjo*. He had heard it was a cynical attack on evangelical Christianity. But after Jones saw the film, "He reversed his recommendation and instructed the people not to see it." Undoubtedly, Jones was afraid he might be implicated by his own resemblance to the crooked evangelist.

Endlessly haranguing them with his ideas, Jones cut the people off from any ideas but their master's. He used the radio, audiotapes, bulletins, papers, brochures, and tracts to saturate his followers with his own thoughts. And eventually any idea contradictory to Jones's had little chance of breaking through the wall of words he had constructed.

The restrictions imposed in California upon what people could know about the world were of course only a mild prelude to the restrictions later imposed in Guyana. Yolanda Crawford, who managed to talk her way out of Jonestown in 1977, said that Jones was telling his Jonestown flock that the fascist takeover had already begun in the United States. In an affidavit filed in April 1978 (*see* Appendix 2), she reported: "Jim Jones said that black people and their sympathizers were going to be destroyed, that 'the Ku Klux Klan is marching in the streets of San Francisco, Los Angeles, and cities back east,' [and that] 'the drought in California is so bad, Los Angeles is being deserted.' "

Emotional Isolation

With his followers exhausted and cut off from the flow of fresh ideas, Jones set about isolating them emotionally. As several Concerned Relatives of Jonestown residents put it in an affidavit (appendix 1), "Jones used psychological coercion as part of a mind-programming campaign aimed at destroying family ties, discrediting belief in God and causing contempt for the United States of America." Imagine how it would feel to be isolated from your family and friends, isolated from God, and isolated from your homeland and its people!

I have already illustrated how Jones broke up marriages, dissolved family units, and shifted children from one home to another; interfered in friendships; cut off budding romances, and created fear and suspicion by one member for another; turned people against God, their former churches, and pastors; and convinced them that even the government was their enemy. In that state of emotional isolation, they could talk to no one. Their fear or suspicion or resentment would overpower any conversation and dominate any potential relationship.

Parents who had children in People's Temple saw clearly the effect of Jones's tactics on their children's attitudes. They would try to draw their children into conversation about the church or about Jones and what he believed but would get no response. Open dialogue made the youngsters uneasy and afraid.

Sherwin Harris referred, for example, to the "flora and fauna letters" that he used to get from his daughter, LeAnn. Invariably, they would contain "nothing substantive—the birds and the bees, how beautiful Jonestown is, and all this kind of stuff, but never a complaint." When he finally got a chance to see his daughter in Georgetown (shortly before LeAnn, her mother, Linda Sharon Amos, and her sisters died of slashed throats), he found her willing to talk about anything but the church. When that subject came up, she would say, "It distresses me to talk about that, Dad. Let's have a nice visit."

Jones told truths, half-truths, and lies to create this sense of emotional isolation, and children were by no means alone in succumbing. Clare Bouquet, a Concerned Relative who visited Guyana with the Ryan party, cited one example of Jones's lies and their effectiveness. She told me, "During the performance they gave Friday night for Ryan and his party, one of the survivors said she was sitting next to this nice woman, who was one of the visitors. They were chatting, and the survivor discovered to her dismay that this nice lady she was chatting with was that horrible monster, Beverly Oliver. She was shocked because Beverly Oliver, as a Concerned Relative, had been described to her as such a horrible monster. And here's this nice lady, that she's sitting there enjoying the party with who has come to see her sons."

Jones did make one small exception. He did want people to keep some relationships partially alive. Yolanda Crawford explained, "[Jones] said that our highest and only loyalty should be 'the cause,' and that the only reason for staying in touch with our families was to collect inheritances when 'they died off' and to keep them pacified 'so as not to make trouble for the cause.' "

Jones apparently succeeded in fostering a state of mind in which his followers could believe and relate to no person or institution other than Jones. He took those already-fragile psyches that passed the screening process at the Temple. He exhausted them. He blocked their free access to ideas. And then he actively undermined relationships.

Physical Isolation

Ross Case, one of Jones's associate pastors in Indianapolis, who defected before Jones moved to Redwood Valley, said, "Jones could simply not allow any expressions of loyalty between people other than himself." Temporal, intellectual, and emotional isolation was not enough to guarantee Jones's total hold on his congregation. So, he also used physical isolation to control them.

Even before Jonestown, physical intimidation was widely used to keep his followers afraid to leave the cult. Often I think of Al Mills's words, quoted earlier: "In making the decision to leave, you had to decide you would rather die than go back to another meeting, because there was the threat of death if you left." Today, weeks after the Jonestown massacre, I have seen former members carry loaded revolvers in case they should meet up with any of Jones's "angels," as he so euphemistically described the henchmen who would carry out his threats.

When the press began reporting the bizarre and tyrannical practices taking place in the Temple, including at least two suspicious suicides, Jones fled to Jonestown. There he joined the hundreds of others he had already induced to go to Guyana with the promise of utopia and the threat of a fascist takeover back home. It is in Jonestown that physical isolation became especially important. Whereas it had previously been a serious risk to leave the Temple against Jones's will, now it was a virtual impossibility. Debbie Blakey, one of Jones's top aides, said that Jonestown "was swarming with armed guards. No one was permitted to leave unless on a special assignment, and those assignments were given only to the most trusted.'' She was one of those who were trusted enough to leave, which is why she is alive today. She defected in May 1978.

Nine hundred and twelve others did not escape. But now it is easier for me to understand why. Jonestown is a perfect example of Jones's use of isolation as a means of control. *Temporal isolation:* They worked day and night to keep the jungle from growing over them. *Intellectual isolation:* In that rustic compound six thousand miles from home there was one short-wave radio to connect them to the news and views of the world outside, and Jones controlled the radio. *Emotional isolation:* They sat side by side in the dining hall. They slept side by side in the barracks. They played side by side on the grassy field. But they were afraid of each other and cut off from the natural relationships that might have given them life. *Physical isolation:* Jones's guards patrolled the camp's perimeters. Jones's guns and Jones's lies kept the people afraid.

Given insight into this awful and total state of isolation, isn't it easier to understand why that great crowd obeyed when Jones's voice echoed over the jungle, ''Alert! Alert! Everyone to the pavilion!''? Isn't it getting clearer why they looked on numbly when the nurses squirted poison down their children's throats? Isn't it more obvious why they lined up, dipped their little paper cups into the vat of poison—and died? There may have been only one suicide in Jonestown. Jones's followers were murdered by the man who promised to give them life.

For Reflection and Discussion

1. What factors in your own life keep you most isolated from information? from other people?
2. In what ways does your church encourage isolation from other groups or certain activities or ideas? Do you think a certain sort of isolation is ever justified? Why or why not? (Consider, for instance, God's command to Israel that it be separate from other nations; and *see* 2 Corinthians 6:14.)
3. Read the whole of Ephesians chapter 4, giving particular attention to verse 14. List the factors mentioned in this chapter that support a healthy community, and reflect upon them. Where do you see the most need for improvement in your own church or fellowship group?

Scripture Texts

2 Corinthians 6:14
Do not be mismated with unbelievers. For what partnership have righteousness and iniquity? Or what fellowship has light with darkness?

Ephesians 4:14
That we may no longer be children, tossed to and fro and carried about with every wind of doctrine, by the cunning of men, by their craftiness in deceitful wiles.

9

Why So Few People Escaped the Cult

By Jonestown, it was too late.

I have read and reread the hundreds of typed pages of manuscripts from my interviews with defectors and survivors and parents. I have collected a pile of data a foot high on Jones and the People's Temple. And I am beginning better to understand how he deceived them. But I must ask the question one more time. Why didn't they get out? Why did they follow him as sheep to that final, awful slaughter?

For Some, Jonestown Was Not That Bad

Do you remember the letter someone found on Jones's body? The primitive scrawl and syntax indicate it was not from one of Jones's elite, but from one of the workers. "Dear Dad," the person wrote, "You have given me all the life I've ever had." This is the one truth from Jonestown that we Christians will probably never deal with honestly; and yet it is the fact we need most to face. The majority of those who died at Jonestown were poor and uneducated and black. They once lived in the ghettos; and all most of us know about the ghetto is what we see as we drive quickly through it on elevated freeways. Apparently the life they had there was no less a prison than the horror and hopelessness of Jonestown.

Before we shake our heads again and wonder why the mass of them didn't get out of Jonestown before the massacre, we have to admit that many of them had no place worth going. Jones gave them *false* hope, but at least it was hope. Wayne Pietila remembers those large meetings in San Francisco and Los Angeles when Jones was doing his preacher-man miracle show. He says, "They came to Jones mostly to be healed. They were black and downtrodden—the oppressed people of the United States. They were religious, but they didn't really care what he said. They were sick and they heard that Jones could heal them. And so they came."

"And you have no idea the power that Jones wielded over those people," adds Tim Stoen, "how charismatic he was, how he attracted people. Once I watched him throw his arms around a lonely, old, black woman. The way she looked up at him made me cry."

"Even Jim Jones's mortal enemies said at the beginning Jones did a lot of good," says Clare Bouquet, whose son died with Jones in the jungle. "I think Jones was a kook from the day he was born, but he did have some good things going, like his rehabilitation program with drug addicts and alcoholics and juvenile delinquents.''

So many of those who died were victims of the evil at work in our society. No matter how we hate Jones's lies, we have to concede that one reason many of them may have taken the poison is that life with us was not all that much better than death with Jones in the jungle.

Others Saw the Truth But Excused It

The more people I interview, the more sure I am that almost every one of Jones's followers, except perhaps the very old and the very young, had some indication early in his association with People's Temple that something was wrong with Jones and his church. But almost everyone had a way to justify the wrong he saw and remain silent about it—at least at first.

Remember Wayne Pietila's words: "The religious ones came for healing. They didn't really care what he said." Yet Grace Stoen had quite the opposite reaction: "I never believed in the healing. I was always skeptical about that. But when we first entered the church, I'll never forget seeing total integration for the first time. There were all races there. There were middle-class and lower-class, educated and illiterate. I was really touched by the warmness of the people."

As one defector confessed, "I tolerated the religious side because there was a good thing going on—a humanitarian thing. Jones was using the religious stuff as a means to an end. He knew religious people are already sensitive and have feeling for the human situation. They have right ideas about freedom and race, so these were the people that Jim was trying to get in through religion; and we just kind of smiled down the religious thing."

Al Mills confesses, "I gradually became aware that there were some phony healings, but I also felt that some of them were real. Tim Stoen added, "When I love somebody, I'm blind to faults and I'll champion him against all other odds, which I did with Jones, even though part of me knew that things were getting out of control. If I had known the cancer cures were false, I probably would have continued with him still." In fact, Jones himself gave hints the cures were rigged. As Stoen commented in one interview, "Jones would say, 'How many of you would be deeply offended if I occasionally had to *dramatize'* — that's the word he used—'a healing in order to create the faith necessary to have people healed?' "

Wayne Pietila summarizes why so many rationalized the phony healings: "What I believe is that when you get enough people in a room together and everyone holds hands and thinks positive thoughts, then I believe there is a force among you that would help somebody stand straighter, if he were crippled, and if she were hurting, she would start feeling better again."

Even when Jones was beating people mercilessly and "laughing with sadistic joy," the rationalizing continued. Al Mills remembers thinking, "Am I going to let a little whipping stand in the way of the total picture? Jones isn't perfect, but he is the only one that can hold this group together; and this group is going to do great things in this world to make it a better place."

Tim Stoen said, "Sometimes I would see a beating and it was very distasteful; but I figured, *Look, I'm a lawyer; and if anybody ever really got hurt, I would know, because there would be a hospital report, a doctor's report.* Nothing like that ever came through. That's how I rationalized it in my mind. Jones knew I was squeamish. My wife told me that Jim didn't want me coming to the meetings. I was the only one excused. He got what he wanted from me. And I, Tim Stoen, neglected my moral responsibility to investigate when I should have investigated. Okay, I admit to that."

Others Saw the Truth But Were Afraid to Tell It
In the case of the People's Temple, it was more than rationalizing that kept the people silent. There was a small arsenal of weapons found at Jonestown. Were they used to protect the people from jungle animals, or were they used to keep the people fearful and in line? Clare Bouquet, who accompanied Ryan's party to Georgetown, said, "He had them believing the jungle was full

of mercenary soldiers who would kill them if they went beyond the perimeter.'' Sherwin Harris, another Concerned Relative who went with the Congressman on that last trip to South America, heard that Jones told his followers that the Guyanese government had given him permission to shoot anyone who tried to escape.

Harris said, "Jones told them anything. He made them believe that he had complete control over their lives. He made himself to be the master of their lives and the master of their death." In Debbie Layton's prophetic warning (which we have printed in Appendix 3) she told the world that Jones took the people's passports—but nobody would believe her. Now everyone has seen the large, locked trunk, filled with passports.

Jones created a world of fear at his Temple. Long before Jonestown, Al Mills remembers, "He had us all believing we would be killed if we were traitors." Daphene Mills, only a small child, was fearful because she remembers, "He told us he could read our minds. So every time I had any suspicions about him, like maybe he's not really God, or maybe everything he says is fake, then I'd start thinking, *But if he can read my mind, I better shut up quick.*"

Jones used parents against their children. Daphene says, "I always dreamed about getting out, but they kept me in line through my mother. They just told my mother all the bad things I did and then she would punish me." When

Daphene's parents tried to defect, Jones reversed the strategy and turned the children against their parents. "As soon as Jones got our letter," remembers Daphene's mother, "he immediately contacted all our kids and took them into a big 'I love you' strategy meeting. He told them, 'Your parents are going the way of the devil.' He just totally brainwashed our kids against us."

On one occasion Jones even used a death in the congregation to add to the growing state of fear. Grace Stoen reports, "One of the most powerful tools that Jones used to get people to the church and keep them there, especially the black, older people, was that they would never die as long as they were with him. He promised to bring them back from death. He promised to heal them. Then in 1975 when someone did die, it was all hush-hush, and Jones let the idea circulate that the reason the person died was that the dead one was thinking about leaving People's Temple." So the people's judgment was bent by their needs and fears, as well as by their rationalizations.

The result was that every member of the People's Temple participated in the deception in one way or another. To drive home the point, let's take a closer look at Jones's miracle stories. Responsibility cannot be limited to Jones and his henchpeople, who consciously manufactured miracle stories to deceive. Others, like Stoen and Pietila, who got caught up and excused Jones's manufactured miracles because they felt people needed them "to boost their faith," or "to give their offerings," had a vital part in maintaining the illusions. And so did that third group who, in their innocence and naïveté, simply repeated the miracle stories, believing them, and needing them to be true. They never stopped to ask the questions that might have uncovered the deception and saved almost a thousand lives.

Miracle stories are the stock and trade of contemporary Christianity. Offerings and appeal letters feature miracle stories that moved people to give. Many popular Christian books, films, records, television programs retell miracle stories to boost Christian faith. Instant Christian celebrities are created and widely heard because of some miracle God has wrought in their lives. Even in small groups and in intimate conversation, we Christians tend to share only the miracle side of the faith. We do it to encourage each other, and to keep our standing in the community. It is much harder for us, publicly or privately, to be really honest about the struggle side of faith, the doubt side, the failure and forgiveness side.

The insistence on maintaining a positive façade has as disastrous a potential for evil as the manufactured miracles of Jones. It is a deception to imply that being born again is a cure-all for the difficult problems and decisions that face us. It is a deception to testify to our wonderful conversion, without ever telling the truth about the long days and nights that followed. It is a deception to

pretend even to our most intimate friends that we
are always living the Christian life victoriously.
Ignorance of both sides of the story can lead to
loss of faith, disillusionment, and even death.

Out of Jonestown come the questions: Are we,
like Jones, guilty of manufacturing, embellishing,
and exaggerating miracle stories to keep our good
standing in a religious community, or even to
save that community's good cause? Are we, like
the second group of Temple members, guilty of
going along with the half-truths because the
people need a "faith boost" or a "nudge to giving"? Are we part of that third group, hearing and
repeating the miracle stories blindly, even though
our own experience testifies that there is another
side to Christian truth as well?

Jonestown reminds us how easy it is to be
caught up in a fatal deception. And no matter how
innocent or well meaning our participation in that
deception has been, it needs to stop. Jonestown
warns us, too, how difficult and painful it is to
confess our own failures, let alone confront in
love and even condemn those who would go on
deceiving.

Tim Stoen and the other defectors I have interviewed may have suspected and even known the
truth and failed to report it; but before we judge
them, let's remember how much they have tried
to do to undo the wrong. They spent every available hour of their time begging people to take
their warnings about Jones seriously. They have

practically bankrupted themselves in the courts, traveling to government centers, establishing the Human Freedom Center, flying back and forth to Guyana trying to stop Jones before it was too late. They, at least, have been honest about their error, have stopped rationalizing it, have set personal fears aside, and have done everything possible to make up for it.

A Few Tried to Criticize Him

The fact remains that in spite of all the pressures to remain silent, there were those who tried to confront Jones before they left the Temple. There were still people in the Temple who, at great personal risk, tried to speak honestly and frankly to him, but even these seldom succeeded. Wayne Pietila remembers one of the tricks Jones played to discourage such frankness. "He'd have a heart attack. He would stage an actual heart attack. He had large tanks of oxygen standing by, and his nurses would rush to him, stick a mask on him and work to revive him—to save his life. Imagine how the critic felt then. *You just killed the boss.* And everybody is looking at you and you really felt the pressure, so you were afraid to say anything after that."

Al and Jeannie Mills tried to get through to Jones in three different ways in the early seventies. Al Mills explained, "Although access to Jones was very difficult, we were told that anyone could write him a note and could expect an answer. When I discovered that Jones was prejudiced against black people in his beatings, I had to tell him. He had given a black girl who stole a dimestore item fifty whacks with the board, and she only stole a comb that she needed. But to a white boy who stole a car, and later a woman's purse, he gave only ten whacks. Since we couldn't criticize Jones publicly, I wrote a letter and gave it to him. I was the Temple photographer and saw him on the platform all the time. One day he said to me, 'Al, you just don't understand'; and that was all the response I got.''

Jean Mills tried another interesting tactic. She was concerned that the beatings were getting extremely cruel. ''Jones was sadistically laughing while children were being beaten, or while senior citizens were boxing one another for punishment,'' explained her husband, ''so Jean made a false confession that she got enjoyment out of seeing small children suffer, hoping that Jones might see himself in her words. In fact, after her confession, Jones admitted that he himself had had sexual desires for some young boy in the church, but it didn't change Jones. In fact, he had the little boy beaten unmercifully in the church not long after that.

''We had submitted several programs to Jones, through the Planning Commission, asking him to please change his strategy, telling him the punishments were unfair,'' recounts Jean. ''Nothing worked. So, one day we even suggested to him that a lot of the biggest movements have a dead God or an absent God—like Buddha and Jesus. We reminded him that some of the greatest leaders had movements that didn't really go places until the leader disappeared, and that perhaps if he would disappear, his movement could get off the ground. We made it very logical; it was a three-page total plan describing how he could go to another country, live in luxury, and run the organization from far away. We were desperate. This man had gone mad and we were trying to salvage the organization. But he didn't want to go. He just said, 'No, the people wouldn't stay in line without me.' When we realized there wasn't any hope of changing him, of salvaging the dream, no way to go back and pick up the utopia we had once, we began our plans to escape.''

Bonnie Thielmann cites the time she tried to confront Jones after he told the congregation they were all homosexuals and lesbians. ''I stood up,'' she said, ''and when I did he went into a rage. His face turned beet-red. He shook his fists at me and said, 'Anarchist, anarchist, my own daughter is an anarchist.' I answered, 'That's a crock,' and the whole congregation around me stood up. They were shaking their fists and saying, 'How dare you go against Father. Father knows everything. How dare you think you know better than he does.' It was awful.''

Bonnie kept trying even after the public shaming. ''I stood in line after the meeting till about

3:00 A.M.'' she remembers. "I had questions only Jones could answer. But how could anybody reach him? We weren't supposed to go to his house. There were guards everywhere. We couldn't call him. So I stood in line. When I finally reached him, he told his guards something like, 'There are no exceptions . . .' and I turned on my heels and ran out of the church. I got in my car and they ran after me. Jones called, 'What is it?' I yelled at him, 'All this *precious daughter* stuff . . . if you can't talk to me when I need you, it's a bunch of garbage' and I just kept going. He said, 'You are going to die.' But I thought, *So what*. We were all so frightened. I didn't know whether they would send somebody to kill me. But that seemed fine. At least I would die in freedom rather than in his captivity.''

By Jonestown it was too late to criticize Jones. He had the majority of his followers so regimented that the members themselves silenced the critics, who might have been their one salvation. Odell Rhodes, Jr., was one of the small number of believers who actually saw the massacre in Jonestown. He remembers one brave, old lady, Christine Miller, who spoke up against the suicide, who tried to confront Jones right up to the end.

Apparently, Rhodes saw Christine swallow hard, brace herself, and then speak firmly to Jones: "I have the right to choose—and I choose not to commit suicide." Apparently there was a stunned silence. Then a wave of hostility against Christine swept the crowd. Jones grew furious, but the old woman stood her ground and asked, "Who made this decision for the children? They didn't have any part of this decision. They have a right to life and happiness."

"Jones told her that with him dead, nobody would be happy," Rhodes said. "Then a wild-eyed woman screeched at Christine, 'When I go, you are going to go before me—because you are going to die!' And a man stood up and snarled, 'Without Jim Jones, you wouldn't have any life anyway!' There was a thunderous chorus of *'Yeah, Yeah!'* After that Jones asked his doctors to bring out the potion. Christine Miller tried to confront him at the end and failed."

It was not easy to leave the Temple.

For Reflection and Discussion

1. Are you basically satisfied with your present life? What gives you hope? What do you do when you are tempted to despair?

2. What sorts of things would you feel unable to discuss in your church or fellowship group?

3. Have you ever confronted anyone (a peer or a person in a superior position) whom you believed to be engaging in wrongdoing? Why not? or what happened? (*See* Matthew 18:15–17.)

4. Ponder/discuss what happened in Jonestown— and what happens among us every day—in the light of these Scriptures: Romans 1:28, 29; 3:10, 13–17; Hebrews 3:13.

Scripture Texts

Matthew 18:15–17
If your brother sins against you, go and tell him his
fault, between you and him alone. If he listens to
you, you have gained your brother. But if he does
not listen, take one or two others along with you,
that every word may be confirmed by the evidence
of two or three witnesses. If he refuses to listen, tell
it to the church; and if he refuses to listen even to the
church, let him be to you as a Gentile and a tax
collector.

Romans 1:28, 29
And since they did not see fit to acknowledge God,
God gave them up to a base mind and to improper
conduct. They were filled with all manner of wickedness, evil, covetousness, malice. Full of envy,
murder, strife, deceit . . . .

Romans 3:10, 13–17
"None is righteous, no, not one . . . they use their
tongues to deceive. The venom of asps is under their
lips. Their mouth is full of curses and bitterness.
Their feet are swift to shed blood, in their paths are
ruin and misery, and the way of peace they do not
know."

Hebrews 3:13
But exhort one another every day . . . that none of
you may be hardened by the deceitfulness of sin.

10

How Defectors Made It to Freedom

Six Steps to Escape

There were only two eyewitnesses to the massacre at Jonestown who lived to tell the awful story of those last moments of Jones and the People's Temple. Stanley Clayton remembers watching everybody die. "One youngster, Chris Newell, took the poison and went to sit next to the other victims to die. But he didn't die right away. He suffered for thirty minutes. Finally one of the nurses came up and injected more poison into his arm. He fell over dead."

By then Clayton was desperate to escape. "I began to walk around the pavilion," he said, "pretending to say a final good-bye to the security staff, and telling them I'd been asked to count heads to see how many people were left. Quickly, I slipped past the guards and headed for Port Kaituma, thirteen miles away." Odell Rhodes, the other eyewitness, overheard the nurse ask for a stethoscope and volunteered to get it. He hid behind a hut until darkness, then ran for the nearest road, away from the death scene.

Now there are charges and countercharges being made. Did the people take the poison voluntarily? Did Jones murder them all? The fact is that they are dead. By the time Jones had them in an isolated jungle outpost, stripped of faith in anyone but himself, exhausted, isolated, penniless, dependent, and in bondage to him, it was long past the time when escape for most of them was possible. But there were a handful of defectors who made it to freedom over the years before Jonestown, and they give important clues on how to escape the clutches of a cult leader and his brainwashed troops.

They Were Pushed One Step Too Far

It would be wonderful to report that defection from the People's Temple came because people were converted to Christianity, or were convinced by the arguments of their parents or friends. Unfortunately, it is not true. Jones kept his followers too exhausted and afraid, isolated and in bondage to defect on well-reasoned, philosophical grounds. For those defectors I interviewed, the first stage to freedom was initiated inadvertently by Jones himself. At one time or another, he pushed the potential defector too far or too fast or beyond what he or she could or would endure. Some remember a moment of anger or shock or incredulity or provoked resistance that was the first step away from People's

Temple. Others recall a series of excesses that forced them to consider defection.

For Wayne Pietila it was the money. "One night Jones said to us on the Planning Commission, 'We got all of this money. Now, what are we going to do with it?' That," said Pietila, "blew me away. I couldn't believe his words. I had always had the impression it was being used for housing people, to build a hospital, a community. It was a big letdown to find out he had no plans—at least no People's Temple plans—for all these millions we had collected."

For Grace Stoen there was a series of final straws. For one, the constant exhaustion got to her. "One time I worked twenty-eight hours straight," she told me. "I was going to break down. I was grinding my teeth at night. I was trying to sleep on the back of the Greyhound bus to Los Angeles, when Jones slapped me on the back and said, 'Get down there and take care of your child.'" Grace remembers vividly another moment Jones went too far. "He was going to make me sign a paper giving Tim Stoen and Carolyn Layton permission to adopt my son, John. And I said, 'I'm not going to sign any more of your papers. I don't care what they are.' He got up and lifted his hand to hit me, and I said, 'Okay, I'll sign it.'"

For Al Mills it was a series of promises Jones made but did not keep. Jones promised to bring in a world of racial love and equality, but Mills finally realized Jones himself was a racist who discriminated against black members of the Temple. He didn't appoint them to places of leadership. He beat them more viciously than he beat the white offenders. Even Jones's adopted black son accused his father of discrimination; and though little Jones recanted under pressure, Mills began to see that Jones would not make good his promise of interracial love and justice. "Jones also promised to be our loving Father," remembers Mills. "He promised that our children would have a college education, medical care, and plenty of food. He promised everything; but when he wouldn't even feed us after we had given up everything for the Temple and we really were going hungry, I figured 'to heck with it.' "

Jeannie Mills got to the point where she could not stand the beatings any longer. She stayed loyal after her own daughter was beaten seventy-five times, but Jones's increasing cruelty finally went too far. Bonnie Theilmann eventually said *no* to the growingly irrational sexual pronouncements. Although Tim Stoen had extra privileges and therefore was somewhat naïve about many of the excesses other members saw, even he finally realized "that if Jones had made all of these people so unhappy, there had to be something wrong."

Each of the defectors reached a point beyond which they could not go. Each defector found something so unreasonable that it demanded a *no*.

And once that *no* was established firmly in their minds, they had no choice but to try to escape, to leave "the cause," to betray the dream in which they had invested everything they owned, and to face the embarrassment and the losses that would follow. However, Jones also had them believing that it was impossible to escape. Getting over that barrier would be the next significant problem.

They Began to Think That Escape Was Possible

As early as 1973, Grace Stoen remembers Jones talking about mass suicide. Jones said, "We are going to commit suicide, but I'm going to stay alive, so I can tell the story of why we did it, so it won't get misinterpreted."

Jack Beam had been with Jones from the beginning. When he heard Jones suggest they all commit suicide, he answered, "No. I'm not going to kill myself, my daughter, and my wife." Now defectors believe that Jones had Beam voice his doubts so forthrightly, just to test the loyalty of the group. The test backfired. Soon after, eight of Jones's followers left the People's Temple. (Beam was not one of them. He died of poison in Jonestown.)

When those first eight people defected, Grace Stoen remembers thinking to herself, "People *can* actually leave the church." She explained that up to that time she believed it was impossible to leave. "I was scared to death. I thought I was trapped forever. They knew where my parents lived. They threatened death for anybody who left. But then eight people defected, and it was the first time I got it into my head that escape was possible.''

We should not really be surprised that seeing that possibility took so long. Jones was a master of pretense. He went to considerable lengths to persuade everyone that escape was impossible. Clare Bouquet told me, ''He had their passports locked in a trunk. And probably the majority of them didn't realize that you can get an emergency passport if you go to the embassy. Knowing that little bit of information might have saved their lives.''

And Jones robbed them of energy and of will. He created a world of false love and real fear. He built a wall around them, isolating them from each other and from the outside world. He told them that the outside world was in chaos, and that they would be killed or tortured if they returned. He fed them endless lies. We must not insult the memories of the dead by oversimplifying the problems they had to overcome in order to escape. But escape, especially before Jonestown, was possible; and knowing that one fact was the second step to freedom.

They Made Contact With Someone Who Shared Their Questions

Everyone was afraid to talk about his doubts or fears with anyone else, knowing that same person might report them to Jones. But the defectors who escaped had to take the risk. Wayne Pietila noticed at that moment when Jones offered "to meet his sexual needs," one person on the Planning Commission grinned to himself. Riding home in the car that night, that same person laughed and said, "You're going to get it from Father." That grin and the mood of the remark that followed made Wayne believe he could trust the man. They escaped together.

Grace Stoen remembers how another person considering defecting, "told me some stuff that I could get him in trouble with, and I told him some stuff that he could use against me." It was like a password that established they were on the same side. "He said, 'Okay, Grace, I'm leaving and you're welcome to go with me.' "

It really was risky to make contact. On the day of his escape, Wayne confided in a man named Tom, who was watching him take a Temple vehicle to escape in. "While I was talking to Tom, my friends cut his phone line, just in case. I told him, 'I'm not going to hurt the church. I just want to disappear.' He shook my hand. He gave me a hug; and the minute I was gone, he ran to his phone, found it cut, and drove to Redwood Valley to tell Jones."

Despite the risks, every defector I talked to had to establish contact with someone who also had doubts and questions, inside or outside the church, to help him or her develop the perspective and maintain the courage to defect.

They Held Back Some Resources From the Cult

It takes physical, emotional, and financial resources, or access to someone willing to share his resources to escape a cult. Those who followed Jones (who had any money to start with) were robbed right from the beginning. He took their savings accounts, checking accounts, credit cards, property, possessions, bonds, annuities, Social Security checks, and pensions. He had his followers sign blank permission slips Jones could use to steal anything they might gain after leaving the church.

He also cut them off from the emotional resources of former friends and family. He built deep wells of hatred and fear between members and nonmembers. It was not easy for his followers to climb these walls to reestablish relationships, even to escape.

So most of those who finally did manage to escape had resources hidden from Jones and the Temple that made escape possible. The Millses refused to give up their marriage. Remember, when they joined the Temple, they promised each other that Jones would never stop them from talking freely or from making love. In that intimacy, withheld from the grip of the People's Temple, they found the strength to escape. The Millses had given Jones the equity in several homes they owned, but they held back one-half ownership in a home they owned jointly with Jean Mills's mother. So they had physical, psychological, and financial resources stored up for that day when they would escape.

Tim Stoen kept back his privacy. He said to me, "I went to Jonestown and worked in the sawmill. I lived at the level of the people, but I refused to give up my credit cards and a bank account. I needed my privacy. I was hungry for culture. I needed to be nourished. When Jones found I kept back my Visa Card and my retirement account, he accused me of being a CIA agent. He never understood."

Grace Stoen kept back two important friendships with girl friends outside the church. "I would sneak out," she told me, "and meet my friend. I had known her since the third grade . . . . They were the only people I really talked to. It was so important to have someone understand, to say, 'I feel the same way you do.' That's what really got me to leave."

Knowing that the few defectors who escaped the People's Temple had resources (or access to others' resources) made me wonder about our job as Christians to make resources available to those who might be considering escape from other cults. One idea that Tim Stoen suggested was an "800" or toll-free telephone number that any member of any cult could call for immediate understanding and financial aid. Our Christian churches, or even a Christian church in America, could provide that practical service to our brothers and sisters and to anyone else who has been deceived.

They Didn't Give in to Tricks or Terror

Jones had, of course, developed a full bag of tricks to use against those who left or were planning to leave the People's Temple. When Debbie Blakey finally decided to leave Jonestown, Grace Stoen reports that Jones's people "tried every trick they could to stop her: begging, pleading, crying, asking her over and over, 'How could you do this to Father?' " We have already discussed the violence Jones used as well.

There were other, softer techniques to prevent defection. The Millses remember the first time they tried to defect. Jones called them and said, " 'I love you so much. I want you to know that nobody in the church even knows that you've left. I told them you were on a big, important mission for me.' He made it very easy for us to get back in; so, when we returned we were not villains; we were heroes sent on a secret mission for Father; and we came back in better standing than we left."

Bonnie Theilmann recalls a visit from Jones's wife, Marcie, who told her, " 'Bonnie, Jim is very concerned for your life.' I answered her, 'Sure, and if I'm killed in some horrible accident, he will use it to keep everybody else in line.' " Marcie also visited Grace Stoen after her defection. With the visits would come hundreds of cards and letters from other Temple members. *"Please come back. We love you . . . We care about you*. They wrote hundreds of letters; and it really meant something, especially when you never received that much mail from anybody."

When Tim Stoen confessed his need to be nourished outside Jonestown, Jones picked up the hint of defection and used another common technique. (Recall, I quoted earlier this standard guilt trick Jones had used on Stoen.) " 'Tim, see that tree over there? I don't think anybody in the world has the right to enjoy the fruit off that tree until everybody does.' He hit the old guilt button in me, and I said, 'You're right. I'm being selfish. I'm not denying myself. I'll give it another try.' "

Jones even used the children of potential defectors to keep them in the cult. Jean Mills said, "One day our little son, Eddie, came up to us and said, 'Mom, don't you care about what is happening to the world?' 'Of course I care,' I answered. 'Well, what are you going to do about it?' he shot back. I told him his Dad and I would try, but he interrupted with, 'Not if you are not going to our church. We're the only group that can do anything. You can't do anything by yourself.' He was only ten years old."

Fortunately, the defectors I have interviewed eventually refused to be pressured by Jones's tricks and by his terror. But even after they defected, the terror continued. The Millses changed their names and moved away, but the threats still came. "We woke up one morning and there was a threatening note on our back table. A Temple member had committed suicide about that time. They had gone into her home to take everything out that had anything to do with the Temple, and there was a lot of whispering about how she had actually died. I'm still not overly convinced that the girl hanged herself. But the note we found referred to her and said, 'We would hate for what happened to *M*. to happen to you.'

"The way they wrote and delivered their threats was always spooky," continued Mills. "Our doors had been locked, and yet the threatening note appeared on the dining-room table. Jones said he had a mysterious power, and at times like that it was difficult not to believe him. So we checked and checked, until we found someone had climbed in our bathroom window. But we were still afraid that they had poisoned the food or something, so we dumped out everything into the garbage."

The threat of death against Temple defectors continues now after Jones's death. While I interviewed defectors in San Francisco whose secret addresses were known only to the federal marshals assigned to protect them, those same addresses were found in a real-estate office in Los Angeles connected to Jones, along with a cache of bombs and ammunition. The notion of a "hit list" put out by Jones to create fear even after his death is taken quite seriously by federal officials. Tim Stoen is at the top of the list.

He told me, "I speculate that Jones figured if he was going down, he wanted all his money to make a bigger dent for Jim Jonesism on the world. Probably he would send it to the PLO or Black September [two world-wide terrorist organizations] to kill his enemies. I've been expecting it for a year. Every morning I look for dynamite in my exhaust pipe. But like it says in Job, 'That which I fear has come upon me.' I refuse to be afraid. I'm not bravado but I like to live. I alternate my times and routes of travel, but I am not going to have my life dominated by fear. Everybody knows that I'm probably Number One on the hit list. And that is good. Because if people know that I can walk around freely, then they can walk around freely, too. So I say, 'Thank you, Jim Jones, for making me free of fear.' Right?"

They Give Each Other Strength

Al and Jeannie Mills and all those other defectors and friends who founded the Human Freedom Center are working to create a place where other defectors from the Temple and survivors of Jonestown can gather to give each other strength. "It will take a lot of time," says Jean Mills. "Everybody comes out of a nightmare at a different speed. One woman who defected still carried one of Jones's healing cloths for months after she left the Temple. Yesterday a woman finally called

to talk after waiting a year before making contact
with anyone. She was so afraid. We can't rush
anyone. We're still trying to get over it ourselves."

As I sat in the center of the old yellow house on
Regent Street, both phones rang nonstop. Two
coffee pots were constantly being filled and
emptied again. The Millses, Grace Stoen, Holli
Morton and the others sat and talked to anyone
who needed conversation. Everyone was welcome. These people have all been marked to die
on Jones's enemy hit list. Most of them expect
Jones's allies to be as fatally faithful to him now
that he is dead, as they were while he lived. But
they refuse to live in fear.

I remember standing on the front porch with
Jeannie Mills. After I had read about the FBI
reports of the hit list and seen the patrol cars
prowling the neighborhood, I asked her somewhat uncourageously, "Why are we talking out
here on the porch?" She answered, "But that's
what we have to do. As long as we can show
people in cults around the world that we are not
afraid, then fear cannot hold them either."

As I sat and talked to them and wondered what
we could do for them, as they find their way back
to somewhat normal lives, I heard a timid knock
on the front door. When a defector answered it,
expecting another television crew or police official, it was instead a member of the Cabrillo As-
semblies of God Church in Santa Cruz, Califor-

nia. He said, "Our pastor heard you were in need of clothes and food. We have a pickup truck outside with a few things we thought you could use for your defectors and survivors. Where would you like us to deliver them?" There were squeals of delight, as several young defectors heard the news and ran to help unload the truck. "You see," said Jeannie, "someone will come through for us." How glad I was that this first sign of "coming through for them" was from a Christian church.

For Reflection and Discussion

1. Do you have any commitments as complete as that of the People's Temple members? Does Jonestown make you afraid of that sort of commitment? Why or why not?

2. Jesus repeated the demand made in the Old Testament that we love God with *all* our heart, soul, mind, and strength (Mark 12:30). How does that commandment differ from Jones's requirements?

3. If Christ's commandment is absolute, how can we justify holding back any resources so as to protect ourselves from cults? Discuss.

4. What factor(s) could push you to leave your church? What risks would be involved in leaving? What sort of support, if any, would you need?

5. What sorts of pressures were Jesus' disciples under to stay with Him? In what ways, if any, did these pressures differ from those faced by Jones's disciples? (You may wish to review the Gospel narratives with this question in mind.)

Scripture Text

Mark 12:30

"And you shall love the Lord your God with all your heart, and with all your soul, and with all your mind, and with all your strength."

11

It Must Not Happen Again

Eight Resolutions for Each of Us

Will we ever know what really happened in those last five hours at Jonestown? Will we ever really understand Jones's motives or methods? Jeannie Mills described the real problem left to us all. When she heard the news from Guyana, she said, "I was thinking about little Sissy, who had begged to come out and live with us. *Dead.* And little Julie, who sort of spit out the poison and tried to hide the syringe. *Dead.* And the people who begged for help. *Dead.* And the little old people that we knew and loved, who once lived with us. *Dead.* I thought, *This death can't be for nothing. Someone's going to listen now. It's got to have purpose; you've got to make meaning out of it.*"

We Share the Blame

Let's face it. Jones fooled most of us. That's the first lesson we need to learn from Jonestown. Each of us, in his or her own way, is responsible for those who died in the jungle. Jones fooled the politicians we elected: congresspersons, governors, mayors, attorneys general, city councilmen, as well as White House Cabinet members. He fooled the leaders of our churches: officials of the Disciples of Christ, leaders of local, state, and national councils of churches, and associations of evangelicals, local pastors, and lay leaders. He fooled members of State Department: ambassadors, consular officials, governmental bureaucrats on every level. He fooled the FBI and the CIA. He fooled the Internal Revenue Service and the US Postal Service and the Federal Communications Commission. He fooled families and friends of his victims; and he fooled the people who died. Every system designed to prevent this kind of horror failed. Every person assigned to keep watch for us was asleep at his post. Suits and countersuits in national and international courts will rage on for years as attempts to fix the blame proceed. But finally the blame rests with us.

If we deny our guilt, then we guarantee similar disasters will happen again. From San Francisco to Georgetown, Guyana, people on every level of leadership are denying their guilt. And that is why charlatans and demagogues will always have their way. None of us wants to be responsible. Even the church would like a scapegoat.

Blame Karl Irvin, Regional President of the Christian Church (Disciples of Christ)? Tim Stoen, Jeannie Mills, and others had visited Irvin at his regional headquarters office. "We took them every bit of information. Tim Stoen showed them documents and documents and documents, telling what was going on behind closed doors. Karl Irvin did not care," says Mrs. Mills, justifiably angry. "They were told. They were begged. But nobody cared. All they cared about . . . was not getting involved—was keeping the status quo."

Blame the Reverend John Moore, a Methodist superintendent, who supported Jones? "Anytime Jones wanted anything," Jeannie Mills reports (and other defectors confirm)," he [Jones] would say, 'Carolyn, get your dad to do this.' " The defectors claim that Moore is the minister who got an award for Jones—at Jones's request—as one of America's hundred most popular clergymen. Grace Stoen testified that it was Moore who discredited Debbie Blakey's warning about the conditions in Jonestown. (*See* Appendix 3.)

Blame Irvin, if you dare. Isn't it enough that he will never quit wondering. *Could I have stopped the madman before he murdered 912 men, women and children?* Blame Moore, if you want to. But isn't it enough that his two daughters, Carolyn and Annie, died in Jonestown with the others? Really, must we find a scapegoat for the tragedy? Can't we take *our* rightful share of blame? If the victims had found love and purpose in our local churches, Jones could probably never have fooled them in the first place.

When I asked Jeannie Mills to tell what she

thought the churches' response should be, she gave us three practical suggestions: "*First,*" she said, "the churches should accept the responsibility now, and learn to be more loving to their own members. Then they wouldn't need to go out and look for something else. *Second,*" she continued, "the churches and all these religious organizations who ask for money should be willing to open their doors and their books so that the illegitimate sharks and the dishonest, power-hungry people who exploit others could not survive. *Third,*" she concluded, "if the churches would give the people information about cults, open their doors to ex-cult members like me to come in and talk to the people and explain about the cults, we could save a lot of people a lot of grief."

After spending the last month with defectors and survivors of the People's Temple, I have seen again that the local church—yours and mine—is the front line in the war to keep people out of the cults. The battles will be won or lost by how we fight them there. Therefore I have made the following resolutions about my own relationship to my church:

RESOLUTION NUMBER 1

Grace Stoen said, "I went to church until I was eighteen years old . . . and nobody ever befriended me."

I will do my best to help make my church a more loving community to our members and the strangers in our midst.

RESOLUTION NUMBER 2

Al Mills recalled, "The programs of the churches I attended didn't include much of what Jesus was doing; you know, helping the poor and stuff like that?"

I will do my best to help make my church a more caring community to the real human needs of our members and of the poor, the lonely, the under-privileged, the old and the unemployed in our neighborhoods.

The atrium lobby of the Hyatt Regency Hotel in San Francisco was ablaze with holiday lights. A large orchestra played carols and people passing through the lobby joined their voices in the songs of Christmas. I sat across a table from two of the Concerned Relatives who had only recently returned from Georgetown, after narrowly escaping death with Congressman Ryan.

Directly in front of me sat Clare Bouquet. She, Sherwin Harris, and the others had shared in detail what they had suffered during the last six months, trying to get their children out of Jonestown. Now their kids were dead. They had signed petitions, written letters, mailed affidavits to Congress and to state and federal officials and agencies (*see* Appendix 1), visited the press, picketed, demonstrated, traveled back and forth to Guyana, begged local and national church officials to listen, hired attorneys, worked and prayed—and all to no avail.

Clare Bouquet was the mother of Bryan.

Perhaps you remember the picture of Bryan with Congressman Ryan in Jonestown. In chapter 1, I quoted what he said to Ryan the day they both died: "The next time I see my mother, I want it to be at the other end of a rifle." Yet there she sat across the table from me, a bright, attractive, loving woman, obviously committed to her job as a teacher, to her church, and—until a few days before—to rescuing her son from Jones and his jungle prison.

She said to me, "The thing I don't understand about my son's involvement with Jones is that Bryan was always a very strong-willed kid. From the time he was a baby, he bucked authority. For him to surrender his whole life and all his possessions to Jones is beyond my comprehension. I never will understand, of all my kids, how he got into something like that."

It Could Happen to Our Children

The more I talked to defectors and parents of the Jonestown victims, the more I understood Clare Bouquet's confusion. There was no clear pattern emerging as to why these kids had been deceived. What I am left with is the uneasy realization that it could happen to anybody's children—mine and yours included. Naturally, that fact made me want to get ideas from these parents about what they would have done differently in raising their young children, and what I could learn from them about raising my own.

They made suggestions: "Let your kids know they are fantastic human beings." "Ask your children how they feel about things and then respect their feelings." "Help your kids make decisions, even wrong ones. If they don't learn to make wrong decisions, they will never make the right ones either." "Help your children take responsibility for their own lives." "Love your children." "If you are considering divorce, remember, it will affect your kids more than you realize."

When I asked what to do if our children were already deceived, they answered, "Arguments don't help. Books and pamphlets don't help. They are forbidden to read them and too tired to read them anyway." "Just keep loving your kids. Let them know they're always welcome to come home." "Keep contact if you can." "Pray!"

The Millses told me about rescuing their daughter, Linda, from People's Temple a short while before she was scheduled to go to Jonestown. "We weren't allowed any communication with our daughter for a year," they told me. "But we wanted her to know we loved her. We sent her letters. Later we discovered that Jones intercepted them. But we kept on making attempts to let her know we cared. We told her she was always welcome at home. We had a place for her. We sent her a medical card to cover her health-care needs.

"Finally we got a chance to see her at a wed-

ding. Her guard stayed outside, because she
didn't feel dressed up enough. So we sneaked in
beside Linda and hugged her. I said, 'Linda, we
sure love you, honey. Did you get the medical
card?' She said, 'Yeah, Father gave it to me.' And
we asked if there was anything else she needed.
'Do you need money? Do you need clothes? You
know we're concerned for you.' She needed a
tooth fixed and we told her we would pay for it.
We didn't say anything at all against the group.
We just said we had a place for her. Her natural
mother, Zoe, had been doing the same thing; and
one day Linda threw a few clothes together—
quickly, before anyone found out—and left the
cult.

"Linda came home to us within a few hours of
when Patricia Hearst came home to her parents.
It was such a fantastic thing, because our
thoughts had been with Patricia equally as with
Linda, because she was just as much a victim of
the same type of insanity as we had been."

The Millses warned against any frontal attack
to rescue children from the cults; but Grace Stoen
told me, "I used to wish that my parents would
come here and try to get me out . . . . You can't
imagine how afraid Jones was of some of the parents." Sherwin Harris, one of the parents who
tried, said, "We took a risk and we lost." On the
dedication page of this book I quoted Clare
Bouquet's last words to me: "I hope that your

kids can be saved by our kids being slaughtered."

Although there was no easy answer, no consensus of opinion from these parents who have suffered so much, I want to confess a few resolutions I have made about my own children.

RESOLUTION NUMBER 3

Clare Bouquet said, "I had heard a little bit about the Moonies, but that was so remote. I thought my kids would never be sucked into a dumb thing like that."

I will admit that my children, too, are potential victims of the cults.

RESOLUTION NUMBER 4

Sherwin Harris said, "The qualification for membership was a combination of high ideals and misinformation."

I will help my children understand the way cults work to deceive us.

RESOLUTION NUMBER 5

Clare Bouquet said, "When you come right down to it, all traditional religions do some brainwashing . . . ."

I will try to help my children love Christ and follow His teachings, but I will not hide from them the questions, the fears, and the failures my church and I have known in our attempts to follow Him.

One of Jones's supporters, Minnie Smith (a pseudonym), lives in a small apartment in the public-housing project in the industrial city of Richmond. A *Los Angeles Times* reporter found her name on a giving card in the ruins of Jonestown and visited Minnie Smith to find out why she gave money to Jones. "When I send him the money," she said, "he send me this here picture." She picked up a portrait of Jones. On the back is the printed Scripture: THE HARVEST IS GREAT, BUT THE LABORERS ARE FEW. LUKE 10:2. "You know," continued the old, black woman, "I really thought he were a Christian man. He said he doing all these good things, helping people. Said he need donations to help children and old folks. And now," she paused, "after all this! Oh, well, who am I to judge?"

It is one thing for an old, black woman living in a high-rise slum to ask, "Who am I to judge?" It is something else again when a bright young attorney like Tim Stoen says to me, "I never even thought to question that Jones might not be everything he claimed to be."

We Can Help Keep It From Happening Again

Tim Stoen has paid a terrible debt for not asking the hard questions in time. As I reported earlier, the body of his son John Victor, age six, was found next to Jones's body in the jungle. And remember, Stoen is the first victim on Jones's alleged hit list.

I asked Stoen what he would do differently, if

he had those years in the Temple to live over
again. How have his beliefs changed? What does
he value now? His answers were revealing. "*I
believe in the family*," Stoen answered first.
"What I want now is the chance to have a nuclear
family with children. I want to walk my children
in the park. I want to tell them stories . . . That's
where my head's at." And though Stoen believes
a collectivist environment (such as Jones advo-
cated) helped foster a sense of social responsibility in children, he does not believe that the nuclear family can really be replaced. Stoen told me
that a child needs to feel the closeness of his
father and mother, to have their arms wrapped
around him, to have their personal concern.

RESOLUTION NUMBER 6

I think of Stoen's son lying in the jungle and of
his marriage with Grace apparently ruined by
Jones.

**I think about my own family and resolve that I
will guard it. I will take time to be a responsible
husband and father. I will love my wife and children and wrap my arms around them while I can.**

Tim also talked about the church. "I was an
atheist by the time I left the church," he said.
"After leaving Jones I am convinced there is at
least some divine order." It is difficult to know if
Stoen will find his way back to faith again. He
confessed that in a way his present attitude re-

sembles "the old pietistic point of view" that a spiritual experience is how people are made happy and in turn bring happiness to others. But he does not suggest that those embracing such a formula should ignore the questions of "social justice, racial brotherhood, and economic fairness."

Stoen looks back at his evangelical Christian upbringing and says, "I grew up in a hothouse. I never knew any blacks, radicals, or anything like them. I think the church ought to teach every kind of philosophy that a kid is going to face and not be afraid to deal honestly with any of the questions raised. Evangelicals don't have any faith in the ability of people to knowingly discern truth. I am going to expose my kids to everything."

RESOLUTION NUMBER 7

I will do what I can to keep my church from being a hothouse, where children grow up weak and easily deceived. And I will welcome those who, like Tim Stoen, may doubt or disagree, to join me in my search for Christian truth.

As Stoen talked to me about his continuing concern that the church help establish justice, brotherhood, and fairness in the land, he also shared his newfound appreciation for this nation. "I believe in America," he avows. "I practically get on my knees and kiss the earth. Having been around, I love this country very much." But Stoen has some fear about the nation's future. He thinks the government should "take concrete measures to deal with the proliferation of the cults." He hopes that somehow there will be "a whole new understanding of psychological duress on people." He feels that "all the nation's non-profit corporations should be forced to have their books made available for inspection; and they should make regular reports on how they spend their money or else lose their tax-exempt status."

RESOLUTION NUMBER 8

I have not been a very responsible citizen. I have voted without reading the propositions very carefully. I have paid my taxes without caring too much how they were spent. I have obeyed the laws, seldom even questioning them.

After what I've learned from Jonestown, I will try to be a more alert citizen—alert to both the good and to the evil in this land.

Of course, all these resolutions are worthless to those who died in Jonestown. I admit they might be just my way of squirming out from under all the guilt and helplessness I feel. And as the news dies down from the jungle in Guyana, I am afraid I may forget what I have learned from those days in San Francisco. But I must not forget Jonestown, lest my children, too, end up in some jungle, far from our home and family.

The night that 260 children died out there, Sherwin Harris and Clare Bouquet were sitting in a Georgetown hotel room with Bonnie Thielmann. They had just heard their friends and their families were dead. Harris told me he heard a timid knock on the door and when he opened it, five black hotel maids asked politely if they could enter. The women were almost overcome by grief. They stood trembling around these visitors from America who had lost their families and friends in the massacre. One said, "We are sorry." Her eyes filled with tears as she prayed a simple prayer of strength for them. "Then," said Harris, "they were gone."

For those who died and for those who grieve their passing, all we can do is say, "We, too, are sorry." And then—kneel to pray a prayer of strength for all of us.

Some Reflection and Discussion

1. Consider the *Resolutions* listed in this chapter. How do they apply to you? Are there others you would add?

2. We are not without scriptural warning that many will try to deceive us. Read with care Matthew 24:5–12, 23–27; 2 Thessalonians 2:1–12 and 2 Timothy 3:1–13, and reflect on them with Jones—and yourself and your community—in mind. (These are, indeed, passages referring explicitly to the end times. Remember, however, that Christians are supposed always to live as if they were in the last days.)

3. Look back at your answers to the questions following the Introduction. Would you answer those questions any differently now?

Scripture Texts

Matthew 24:5–12, 23–27

''For many will come in my name, saying, 'I am the Christ,' and they will lead many astray. And you will hear of wars and rumors of wars; see that you are not alarmed; for this must take place, but the end is not yet. For nation will rise against nation, and kingdom against kingdom, and there will be famines and earthquakes in various places: all this is but the beginning of the birth-pangs. Then they will deliver you up to tribulation, and put you to death; and you will be hated by all nations for my name's sake. And then many will fall away, and betray one another, and hate one another. And many false prophets will arise and lead many astray. And because wickedness is multiplied, most men's love will grow cold . . . .

''Then if any one says to you, 'Lo, here is the Christ!' or 'There he is!' do not believe it. For false Christs and false prophets will arise and show great signs and wonders, so as to lead astray, if possible, even the elect. Lo, I have told you beforehand. So, if they say to you, 'Lo, he is in the wilderness,' do not go out; if they say, 'Lo, he is in the inner rooms,' do not believe it. For as the lightning comes from the east and shines as far as the west, so will be the coming of the Son of man.''

2 Thessalonians 2:1–12

Now concerning the coming of our Lord Jesus
Christ and our assembling to meet him, we beg you,
brethren, not to be quickly shaken in mind or ex-
cited, either by spirit or by word, or by letter pur-
porting to be from us, to the effect that the day of the
Lord has come. Let no one deceive you in any way;
for that day will not come, unless the rebellion
comes first, and the man of lawlessness is revealed,
the son of perdition, who opposes and exalts himself
against every so-called god or object of worship, so
that he takes his seat in the temple of God, proclaim-
ing himself to be God. Do you not remember that
when I was still with you I told you this? And you
know what is restraining him now so that he may be
revealed in his time. For the mystery of lawlessness
is already at work; only he who now restrains it will
do so until he is out of the way. And then the lawless
one will be revealed, and the Lord Jesus will slay
him with the breath of his mouth and destroy him by
his appearing and his coming. The coming of the
lawless one by the activity of Satan will be with all
power and with pretended signs and wonders, and
with all wicked deception for those who are to
perish, because they refused to love the truth and so
be saved. Therefore God sends upon them a strong
delusion, to make them believe what is false, so that
all may be condemned who do not believe the truth
but had pleasure in unrighteousness.

2 Timothy 3:1–13

But understand this, that in the last days there will
come times of stress. For men will be lovers of self,

lovers of money, proud, arrogant, abusive, disobedient to their parents, ungrateful, unholy, inhuman, implacable, slanderers, profligates, fierce, haters of good, treacherous, reckless, swollen with conceit, lovers of pleasure rather than lovers of God, holding the form of religion but denying the power of it. Avoid such people. For among them are those who make their way into households and capture weak women, burdened with sins and swayed by various impulses, who will listen to anybody and can never arrive at a knowledge of the truth. As Jannes and Jambres opposed Moses, so these men also oppose the truth, men of corrupt mind and counterfeit faith; but they will not get very far, for their folly will be plain to all, as was that of those two men.

Now you have observed my teaching, my conduct, my aim in life, my faith, my patience, my love, my steadfastness, my persecutions, my sufferings, what befell me at Antioch, at Iconium, and at Lystra, what persecutions I endured; yet from them all the Lord rescued me. Indeed all who desire to live a godly life in Christ Jesus will be persecuted, while evil men and imposters will go on from bad to worse, deceivers and deceived.

Appendix 1

The families of Temple members in Jonestown were concerned for the health and safety of their loved ones. These Concerned Relatives tried desperately to reason with Jones and to warn United States and Guyanese officials of what Jones was doing. They sent the following affidavit to government and church leaders in both countries. Everyone ignored it but one: Congressman Leo Ryan.

ACCUSATION OF HUMAN RIGHTS VIOLATIONS BY REV. JAMES WARREN JONES AGAINST OUR CHILDREN AND RELATIVES AT THE PEOPLES TEMPLE JUNGLE ENCAMPMENT IN GUYANA, SOUTH AMERICA

TO: REV. JAMES WARREN JONES
From: Parents and relatives of children and adults under your control at "Jonestown," Northwest District, Cooperative Republic of Guyana
Date: April 11, 1978

I. INTRODUCTION

We, the undersigned, are the grief-stricken parents and relatives of the hereinafter-designated persons you arranged to be transported to Guyana, South America, at a jungle encampment you call "Jonestown." We are advised there are no telephones or exit roads from Jonestown, and that you now have more than 1,000 U.S. citizens living with you there.

We have allowed nine months to pass since you left the United States in June 1977. Although certain of us knew it would do no good to wait before making a group protest, others of us were willing to wait to see whether you would in fact respect the fundamental freedoms and dignity of our children and family members in Jonestown. Sadly, your conduct over the past year has shown such a flagrant and cruel disregard for human rights that we have no choice as responsible people but to make this public accusation and to demand the immediate elimination of these outrageous abuses.

II. SUMMARY OF VIOLATIONS

We hereby accuse you, Jim Jones, of the following acts violating the human rights of our family members:

1. Making the following threat calculated to cause alarm for the lives of our relatives: "I can say without hesitation that we are devoted to a decision that it is better even to die than to be constantly harassed from one continent to the next."

2. Employing physical intimidation and psychological coercion as part of a mind-programming campaign aimed at destroying family ties,

discrediting belief in God, and causing contempt for the United States of America.

3. Prohibiting our relatives from leaving Guyana by confiscating their passports and money and by stationing guards around Jonestown to prevent anyone escaping.

4. Depriving them of their right to privacy, free speech, and freedom of association by:

a. Prohibiting telephone calls;

b. Prohibiting individual contacts with "outsiders";

c. Censoring all incoming and outgoing mail;

d. Extorting silence from relatives in the U.S. by threats to stop all communication;

e. Preventing our children from seeing us when we travel to Guyana.

The aforesaid conduct by you is a violation of the human rights of our loved ones as guaranteed by Article 55 of the United Nations Charter, and as defined by the Universal Declaration of Human Rights (adopted by the U.N. General Assembly on December 10, 1948). It is also a violation of their constitutional rights as guaranteed by the Constitution of the United States, and as guaranteed by the Constitution of the Cooperative Republic of Guyana (adopted May 26, 1966).

III. THREAT OF DECISION TO DIE

On March 14, 1978 you, Jim Jones, caused to be written on Peoples Temple stationery a letter "to all U.S. Senators and Members of Congress"

complaining of alleged "bureaucratic harassment" and ending with this chilling threat:

> "[I]t is equally evident that people cannot forever be
> continually harassed and beleaguered by such tac-
> tics without seeking alternatives that have been pre-
> sented. I can say without hesitation that we are de-
> voted to a decision that it is better even to die than to
> be constantly harassed from one continent to the
> next."

[A copy of the letter was attached].

We know how exact you are in choosing your
words, and there is little doubt that this letter was
dictated by you personally since it has been your
policy over the years to dictate all letters sent to
governmental officials on Temple stationery.
Your letter seeks to mask, by the use of irrelevant
ideological rhetoric, its real purpose, which is to
divert the attention of U.S. Governmental agencies towards your abuses of human rights by putting them on the defensive.

The "1,000 U.S. citizens" you claim to have
brought to Guyana include our beloved relatives
who are "devoted to a decision that it is better
even to die." We frankly do not know if you have
become so corrupted by power that you would
actually allow a collective "decision" to die, or
whether your letter is simply a bluff designed to
deter investigations into your practices. There is
supporting evidence for our concern in the
affidavit of Yolanda Crawford [*see* appendix 2],

which shows that you have publicly stated in Guyana that you would rather have your people dead than living in the United States, and that you have solicited people to lay down their lives for your cause. You certainly have been successful in making us fearful as to your intentions.

We hereby give you the opportunity now to publicly repudiate our interpretation of your threat. If you refuse to deny the apparent meaning of your letter, we demand that you immediately answer the following questions:

1. When you refer to "a decision that it is better even to die than to be constantly harassed," has this "decision" already been made or is it to be made in the future? If made, when and where? Were our relatives consulted? Did anybody dissent? By what moral or legal justification could you possibly make such a decision on behalf of minor children?

2. When you say you are "devoted" to this decision, does that mean it is irreversible? If irreversible, at what point will the alleged "harassment" have gotten so great as to make death "better"? Would it be an International Human Rights Commission investigation, or an on-premises investigation of your operations by the U.S. government? Who besides you will decide when that point "to die" is reached?

We know your psychological coercion of the residents of Jonestown to be so "totalitarian" that nobody there, including adults, could possi-

bly make such a decision to die freely and voluntarily. The evidence is that our relatives are in
fact hostages, and we hereby serve notice that
should any harm befall them, we will hold you
and Peoples Temple church responsible and will
employ every legal and diplomatic resource to
bring you to justice.

IV. MIND-PROGRAMMING AND INTIMIDATION

The affidavit of Steven A. Katsaris [attached to
the affidavit] is a personal account of his experiences in Guyana. It reveals the terrifying effect of
your mind-programming on his daughter, a bright
24-year old, which has caused her to deny belief
in God, to renounce family ties, and to manifest
symptoms of sleep-deprivation and a serious personality change.

Yolanda Crawford's affidavit [*see* appendix 2]
(Exhibit B) is an eye-witness account of your activities in Guyana by someone present with you.
The affidavit shows that you, Jim Jones, preach
there the following doctrines: a) that you are God
and there is no other God, b) that the United
States is the "most evil" nation in the world, c)
that allegiance to your cause must replace family
loyalty and that parents should be handled at a
distance for the sole purposes of collecting inheritances for the cause and of getting them not to
cause trouble.

The evidence also shows that you have instituted the following practices in Guyana: a) a centralized chain of command whereby all decisions of significance are to be made by you and once made, must be followed by Temple members under threat of punishment; b) the stationing of guards around Jonestown to prevent persons from escaping; and c) the use of degrading punishments (for example, eating hot peppers), sleep-deprivation, food-deprivation, hard labor, and other coercive techniques commonly used in mind-programming.

The evidence also shows that you, Jim Jones, confiscate the passports and monies of people upon their arrival in Guyana, prohibit individual contacts with "outsiders," censor incoming and outgoing mail, prohibit telephone calls by Temple members when in Georgetown, and require Temple members to travel in groups. Ms. Crawford's affidavit also shows that you have publicly threatened that anyone who tries to leave the "cause" will be killed.

The aforesaid conduct by you is a wanton violation of the human rights of our loved ones. It is also a violation of their constitutional rights. The physical intimidation is a violation of the penal codes of the United States and the Cooperative Republic of Guyana.

V. THE HUMAN RIGHTS BEING VIOLATED

We hereby bring to your attention, Jim Jones, the particular provisions which guarantee human rights and constitutional rights that you are violating:

1. *Confiscation of Passports.* Your systematic confiscation of passports and all of the monies of Temple members upon their arrival in Guyana is for the purpose of preventing them from leaving and returning to the United States. You are thereby violating Article 13, Section 2 of the Universal Declaration of Human Rights, which reads:

> "Everyone has the right to leave any country, including his own, and to return to his country."

Your conduct is also a violation of Article 14 (1) of the Constitution of the Cooperative Republic of Guyana, which reads:

> "No person shall be deprived of his freedom of movement, that is to say, the right to move freely throughout Guyana . . . the right to leave Guyana . . . ."

2. *Prohibiting Telephone Calls.* You systematically tell all Temple members upon their arrival in Georgetown, Guyana that they are not permitted, under threat of punishment, to make any telephone calls to family members in the United States or elsewhere, your purpose being to prevent negative information being imparted to relatives in the U.S. Your additional purpose is to overcome the bonds of family which might induce a Temple member to wish to return to his home in

the U.S. This conduct is a violation of Article 19 of the Universal Declaration of Human Rights, which states:

"Everyone has the right to freedom of opinion and expression; this right includes freedom to hold opinions without interference and to seek, receive and impart information and ideas through any media and regardless of frontiers."

This conduct is also a violation of Article 12 (1) of the Guyana Constitution, which reads:

"Except with his own consent, no person shall be hindered in the enjoyment of his freedom of expression, that is to say, freedom to hold opinions without interference, freedom to communicate ideas and information without interference and freedom from interference with his correspondence."

3. *Prohibiting Contacts With Outsiders.* You systematically require that all Temple members, while in Georgetown, not communicate or visit with "outsiders" and not leave the communal headquarters (41 Lamaha Gardens) unless in association with other Temple members. You follow the same policy in Jonestown, enforcing your edicts with guards. Your purpose is to prevent anyone going to the U.S. Embassy and causing them to ask questions how you treat people. Your additional purpose is to discourage Temple members from being exposed to other religions or philosophies, and from viewing their lives inde-

pendent of communal obligations. Your conduct
is a violation of Article 20, Section 2 of the
Universal Declaration of Human Rights, which
states:

"No one may be compelled to belong to an
association." It is also a violation of Article 18 of
the same Declaration, which states:

"Everyone has the right to freedom of thought, conscience and religion; this right includes freedom to
change his religion or belief, and freedom, either
alone or in community with others and in public or
private, to manifest his religion or belief in teaching,
practice, worship and observance."

Your conduct is also a violation of Article 13 (1) of
the Guyana Constitution, which reads:

"Except with his own consent, no person shall be
hindered in the enjoyment of his freedom of assembly and association, that is to say, his right to assemble freely and associate with other persons."

4. *Censoring Mail.* You systematically require
that all of the incoming mail and all of the outgoing mail of Temple members be censored by your
staff. Your purpose is to discourage negative information being "leaked" to people in the U.S.
and to prevent facts about the "outside" world
reaching Temple members which are at variance
with your "party line." This is shown by the
affidavit of Ms. Crawford with respect to the Ku
Klux Klan marching in the streets. Because mail

is the only means of contact available to our loved ones once they are transported to Jonestown, you have thereby effectively cut off all free expression and correspondence. Your conduct is a violation of the right of our relatives to privacy, family, and correspondence under Article 12 of the Universal Declaration of Human Rights, which states:

"No one shall be subjected to arbitrary interference with his privacy, family, home, or correspondence. . . . Everyone has the right to the protection of the law against such interference."

Your censoring of mail is also a violation of Article 12(1) of the Guyana Constitution, which is quoted above.

5. *Extorting Silence From Relatives.* You systematically require that Temple members who write to their family members in the U.S. threaten in their letters that they will stop all further communication if any criticism is made of you or Peoples Temple. For example, Donna Ponts is a 15-year old girl taken to Guyana in July 1977 without her father's knowledge and in violation of a court order requiring her to remain in California unless he gave permission. [Attached to the affidavit was] a letter from Donna to her grandmother which starts out saying: "Grandma, Hi! How are you doing? I hope you and everyone else are doing good." It ends as follows:

"I am sorry to hear that you called the radio station

but since you did I will not be writing you any
more."

Those of us who receive letters from our relatives
in Jonestown find then standardized and unre-
sponsive, as if written by machines. But since it is
all we have, these letters are very precious to us.
You have placed us in the agonizing dilemma of
watching helplessly while the rights of our relatives are violated or losing all contact. We have
chosen, however, not to yield to your extortion,
which is a violation of Article 12 of the Universal
Declaration of Human Rights, quoted above, and
of Article 13(1) of the Guyana Constitution, also
quoted above.

6. *Prohibiting Our Children From Seeing Us.*
Five of the parents who have signed this accusation have travelled from San Francisco some
5,000 miles in order to see their children since you
took them to Guyana. The evidence is clear that
you have instituted a most pernicious campaign
to discredit us in our children's eyes, as can be
concluded from the following experiences:

a. *Steven A. Katsaris.* On September 26, 1977
Steven A. Katsaris arrived in Guyana and at-
tempted to meet with his daughter, Maria. She
was prohibited from meeting with him, duress
being employed by you to force her to lie to the
U.S. Embassy that she did not wish to see her
father because ''he had molested'' her. Mr. Katsaris had with him a letter from Maria inviting him

and saying, "I love you & miss you." On November 3, 1977 Mr. Katsaris returned to Guyana to see his daughter, after first obtaining a promise of assistance from the Guyanese Ambassador to the United States. After days of waiting, Maria was allowed to see her father but only in the presence of three other Temple members. Maria gave evidence of sleep deprivation and a behavior pattern extremely hostile and different from that ever manifested before. For the details of these two visits, refer to [Katsaris affidavit].

b. *Howard and Beverly Oliver.* On December 19, 1977 Howard and Beverly Oliver, together with their attorney Roger Holmes, arrived in Guyana in order to see their two sons, William S. Oliver (age 17) and Bruce Howard Oliver (age 20). In July 1977 both boys had told their parents they were going to Guyana "for two weeks." The Olivers had a court order from a California Superior Court for the return of William. They also had in their possession letters from each son saying "I love you." After spending eight days without success trying to see their sons, they were told that "Jim Jones had a council meeting" and the decision was that "it was best that we did not see or talk to our sons." [Attached was] a handwritten account of Beverly E. Oliver, together with a copy of a letter from each son.

c. *Timothy and Grace Stoen.* On January 4, 1978 Timothy and Grace Stoen arrived in Guyana in connection with habeas corpus proceedings commenced the preceding August. Although they had a California Superior Court order which ordered you to deliver their six-year old child, John Victor Stoen, to them, you refused to let either parent even see their child. The evidence also shows that you have falsely accused Grace as being "unfit" (see Katsaris affidavit) and that on January 18, 1978 three Temple members surrounded Timothy at Timehri Airport in Guyana and threatened his and Grace's lives if they did not drop legal proceedings (see Crime Report made to Guyana Commissioner of Police Lloyd Barker on January 18, 1978).

The aforesaid conduct on your part constitutes a violation of Article 12(1) of the Guyana Constitution, quoted above, and Article 12 of the Universal Declaration of Human Rights, which states as follows:

"No one shall be subjected to arbitrary interference with his . . . family . . . ."

VI. DEMANDS FOR RELIEF

We hereby demand that you, Jim Jones, immediately cease and desist from the aforesaid conduct and that you do the following additional acts immediately:

1. Publicly answer our questions regarding your threat of a collective "decision . . . to die," and publicly promise U.S. Secretary of State Cyrus Vance and Guyana Prime Minister Forbes Burnham that you will never encourage or solicit the death of any person at Jonestown, whether

individually or collectively, for any reason whatsoever;

2. Remove all guards physically preventing our relatives from leaving Jonestown;

3. Return all passports and money taken from our relatives to them for their permanent possession;

4. Permit and encourage our relatives a one-week visit home, at our expense. [Because our relatives have been in Guyana for months (and some, for years) and because it is our belief that they do not know the full Peoples Temple story and have been prejudiced against their families, we demand you demonstrate in practice your contention that they are their own agents by permitting and encouraging our relatives to visit their families in the U.S. for one week, with our guarantee that we will provide them with round trip air fare and not interfere with their return at the end of the family visit should they so choose.]

5. Permit our relatives to write letters to whomever they wish, uncensored and in private.

6. Permit our relatives to read letters sent to them in private and without censorship.

7. Abide by the orders of the courts in the United States which you have heretofore ignored.

8. Notify us within three days on your radiophone network of your full acceptance and compliance with these demands by contacting: Steven A. Katsaris, Trinity School, 915 West Church Street, Ukiah, California 95482; telephone (707)462-8721.

Appendix 2

Yolanda Crawford lived in Jonestown for three months. Her description of the conditions there were ignored by government and church officials in both the United States and Guyana.

AFFIDAVIT OF YOLANDA D. A. CRAWFORD SHOWING THE TEACHINGS AND PRACTICES OF REV. JAMES WARREN JONES IN GUYANA, SOUTH AFRICA.

I, Yolanda D. A. Crawford, certify as follows:

1. I was in Guyana, South America as a member of Peoples Temple from April 1, 1977 until June 29, 1977. Rev. James Warren Jones ("Jim Jones"), the leader of Peoples Temple, was in Guyana most of April and during the latter part of June, at which times I witnessed the following statements and practices by him.

2. Jim Jones said that the United States is the "most evil" nation in the world, referring to its political and industrial leaders as "capitalistic pigs." He said he would rather have his people dead than live in the United States.

3. Jim Jones prior to June said that people would be coming to live in Guyana for a temporary period of time. In June Jim Jones stated that the people he brings over from the United States will be staying in Guyana "permanently."

4. Jim Jones said that nobody will be permitted to leave Jonestown and that he was going to keep guards stationed around Jonestown to keep anybody from leaving. He said that he had guns and that if anyone tries to leave they will be killed ("offed") and their bodies will be left in the jungle and "we can say that we don't know what happened to you." He also said, "I can get a hit man for fifty dollars. It's not hard for me to get a hit man anywhere."

5. While still in the United States, Jim Jones asked the Temple members to turn all their guns over to him. I also saw ammunition being packed in crates for shipment to Guyana addressed to Peoples Temple from San Francisco. I heard Jim Jones say, "If anyone tries to start anything, we are ready and prepared to die for our cause."

6. Jim Jones said that black people and their sympathizers were going to be destroyed in the United States, that "the Ku Klux Klan is marching in the streets of San Francisco, Los Angeles, and cities back east." There was "fighting in the streets, and the drought in California is so bad, Los Angeles is being deserted."

7. Jim Jones said that everyone should turn in their passports and all their money to him, that nobody is to visit any local Guyanese people unless on a "mission" and in the company of other Temple members, that nobody is to make any telephone calls to relatives, that nobody was to send any mail to the United States without first

getting it "cleared." All incoming mail was first received by Temple secretaries and read before being shown to the person addressed.

8. Jim Jones said that "I will lay my body down for this cause" and asked others to make the same promise, which they did by a show of hands, and also asked them to commit themselves to kill anyone attempting to hurt him.

9. Jim Jones ordered all of us to break our ties with families. He said that our highest and only loyalty should be "the cause," and that the only reason for staying in touch with our families was to collect inheritances when "they died off" and to keep them pacified "so as not to make trouble for the cause."

10. Jim Jones ordered us to "report" on one another to prevent "treason." His technique was to have everyone report to him (or his two or three most trusted leaders) all suspicious talk or behavior of others.

11. Jim Jones ordered people punished when they broke his rules. The punishments included food-deprivation, sleep-deprivation, hard labor, and eating South American hot peppers. I saw a teenager, Tommy Bogue, being forced to eat hot peppers at a public meeting.

12. So far as I know, only one person (Leon Brosheard) out of 850 or more residents has dared to leave Jonestown since my mother, husband and I left on June 29, 1977. Before Jim Jones allowed me to leave, I was forced to promise him I would never speak against his church, and that

if I did I would lose his "protection" and be "stabbed in the back." Furthermore, Jim Jones ordered me to sign a number of self-incriminating papers, including a statement that I was against the government of Guyana, that I had plotted against that government, that I was part of the PPP (Peoples Progressive Party), which is the opposition party in Guyana, and that I had come to Guyana to help the PPP. Jim Jones said the reason for signing those papers was to discredit me if I ever decided to leave the movement "and talk." Also, before leaving for Guyana, I was ordered to fabricate a story and sign it stating that I killed someone and threw the body in the ocean. I was told that if I ever caused Jim Jones trouble, he would give that statement to the police. He further intimidated me and others in the congregation by saying, "I, (Jim Jones) have Mafia connections, and they will stand with me all the way."

13. I heard him state to the congregation in Guyana that Marshall Kilduff, who wrote the first articles exposing him, was dead. He said, "The angels have taken care of him." We all knew the "angels" were his people who would do you in if you crossed Jim Jones.

14. Jim Jones ordered all telephone calls to relatives in the United States to be made in the presence of Temple members and after coaching. When my mother tried to call her brother in the United States and get him to stop criticizing the Temple, Jim Jones stood by her side and told her

everything she was to say and then faulted her for not being forceful enough. He ordered us to tell our relatives in the United States to stop criticizing him or we would not be allowed to return home.

15. On numerous occasions I was in the congregation when he told us "I am God" and "there is no other God, and religion is the opium of the people." He stated he used religion only to get to the masses.

16. I recall several instances of Jim Jones stating he could silence critics or defectors by accusing them of being homosexuals, child abusers, terrorists or sexual deviates.

I declare under penalty of perjury that the foregoing is true and correct. Executed at San Francisco, California on April 10, 1978.

Yolanda D. A. Crawford

STATE OF CALIFORNIA
COUNTY OF SAN FRANCISCO

OFFICIAL SEAL
GERALD B. WEINER
NOTARY PUBLIC - CALIFORNIA
SAN FRANCISCO COUNTY
My comm. expires AUG 23, 1981

120 Montgomery St., San Francisco, CA 94104

Appendix 3

Deborah Layton Blakey escaped from Jonestown May 13, 1978. She mailed the following list of accusations to officials in the United States and Guyana. Although her affidavit includes a warning of possible mass suicide, she too was ignored.

AFFIDAVIT OF DEBORAH LAYTON BLAKEY RE THE THREAT AND POSSIBILITY OF MASS SUICIDE BY MEMBERS OF THE PEOPLE'S TEMPLE

I, DEBORAH LAYTON BLAKEY, declare the following under penalty of perjury:

1. The purpose of this affidavit is to call to the attention of the United States government the existence of a situation which threatens the lives of United States citizens living in Jonestown, Guyana.

2. From August, 1971 until May 13, 1978, I was a member of the People's Temple. For a substantial period of time prior to my departure for Guyana in December, 1977, I held the position of Financial Secretary of the People's Temple.

3. I was 18 years old when I joined the People's Temple. I had grown up in affluent circumstances in the permissive atmosphere of Berkeley, California. By joining the People's Temple, I hoped to help others and in the process

to bring structure and self-discipline to my own life.

4. During the years I was a member of the People's Temple, I watched the organization depart with increasing frequency from its professed dedication to social change and participatory democracy. The Rev. Jim Jones gradually assumed a tyrannical hold over the lives of Temple members.

5. Any disagreement with his dictates came to be regarded as "treason." The Rev. Jones labelled any person who left the organization a "traitor" and "fair game." He steadfastly and convincingly maintained that the punishment for defection was death. The fact that severe corporal punishment was frequently administered to Temple members gave the threats a frightening air of reality.

6. The Rev. Jones saw himself as the center of a conspiracy. The identity of the conspirators changed from day to day along with his erratic world vision. He induced the fear in others that, through their contact with him, they had become targets of the conspiracy. He convinced black Temple members that if they did not follow him to Guyana, they would be put into concentration camps and killed. White members were instilled with the belief that their names appeared on a secret list of enemies of the state that was kept by the C.I.A. and that they would be tracked down, tortured, imprisoned, and subsequently killed if they did not flee to Guyana.

7. Frequently, at Temple meetings, Rev. Jones would talk non-stop for hours. At various times, he claimed that he was the reincarnation of either Lenin, Jesus Christ, or one of a variety of other religious or political figures. He claimed that he had divine powers and could heal the sick. He stated that he had extrasensory perception and could tell what everyone was thinking. He said that he had powerful connections the world over, including the Mafia, Idi Amin, and the Soviet government.

8. When I first joined the Temple, Rev. Jones seemed to make clear distinctions between fantasy and reality. I believed that most of the time when he said irrational things, he was aware that they were irrational, but that they served as a tool of his leadership. His theory was that the end justified the means. At other times, he appeared to be deluded by a paranoid vision of the world. He would not sleep for days at a time and talked compulsively about the conspiracies against him. However, as time went on, he appeared to become genuinely irrational.

9. Rev. Jones insisted that Temple members work long hours and completely give up all semblance of a personal life. Proof of loyalty to Jones was confirmed by actions showing that a member had given up everything, even basic necessities. The most loyal were in the worst physical condition. Dark circles under one's eyes or extreme loss of weight were considered signs of loyalty.

10. The primary emotions I came to experience were exhaustion and fear. I knew that Rev. Jones was in some sense "sick," but that did not make me any less afraid of him.

11. Rev. Jones fled the United States in June, 1977 amidst growing public criticism of the practices of the Temple. He informed members of the Temple that he would be imprisoned for life if he did not leave immediately.

12. Between June, 1977 and December, 1977, when I was ordered to depart for Guyana, I had access to coded radio broadcasts from Rev. Jones in Guyana to the People's Temple headquarters in San Francisco.

13. In September, 1977, an event which Rev. Jones viewed as a major crisis occurred. Through listening to coded radio broadcasts and conversations with other members of the Temple staff, I learned that an attorney for former Temple member Grace Stoen had arrived in Guyana, seeking the return of her son, John Victor Stoen.

14. Rev. Jones has expressed particular bitterness toward Grace Stoen. She had been Chief Counselor, a position of great responsibility within the Temple. Her personal qualities of generosity and compassion made her very popular with the membership. Her departure posed a threat to Rev. Jones's absolute control. Rev. Jones delivered a number of public tirades against her. He said that her kindness was faked and that

she was a C.I.A. agent. He swore that he would never return her son to her.

15. I am informed that Rev. Jones believed that he would be able to stop Timothy Stoen, husband of Grace Stoen and father of John Victor Stoen, from speaking against the Temple as long as the child was being held in Guyana. Timothy Stoen, a former Assistant District Attorney in Mendocino and San Francisco counties, had been one of Rev. Jones's most trusted advisors. It was rumored that Stoen was critical of the use of physical force and other forms of intimidation against Temple members. I am further informed that Rev. Jones believed that a public statement by Timothy Stoen would increase the tarnish on his public image.

16. When the Temple lost track of Timothy Stoen, I was assigned to track him down and offer him a large sum of money in return for his silence. Initially, I was to offer him $5,000. I was authorized to pay him up to $10,000. I was not able to locate him and did not see him again until on or about October 6, 1977. On that date, the Temple received information that he would be joining Grace in a San Francisco Superior Court action to determine the custody of John. I was one of a group of Temple members assigned to meet him outside the court and attempt to intimidate him to prevent him from going inside.

17. The September, 1977 crisis concerning John Stoen reached major proportions. The radio

messages from Guyana were frenzied and hysterical. One morning, Terri J. Buford, public relations advisor to Rev. Jones, and myself were instructed to place a telephone call to a high-ranking Guyanese official who was visiting the United States and deliver the following threat: unless the government of Guyana took immediate steps to stall the Guyanese court action regarding John Stoen's custody, the entire population of Jonestown would extinguish itself in a mass suicide by 5:30 P.M. that day. I was later informed that Temple members in Guyana placed similar calls to other Guyanese officials.

18. We later received radio communication to the effect that the court case had been stalled and that the suicide threat was called off.

19. I arrived in Guyana in December, 1977. I spent a week in Georgetown and then, pursuant to orders, traveled to Jonestown.

20. Conditions at Jonestown were even worse than I had feared they would be. The settlement was swarming with armed guards. No one was permitted to leave unless on a special assignment and these assignments were given only to the most trusted. We were allowed to associate with Guyanese people only while on a "mission."

21. The vast majority of the Temple members were required to work in the fields from 7 A.M. to 6 P.M. six days per week and on Sunday from 7 A.M. to 2 P.M. We were allowed one hour for lunch. Most of this hour was spent walking back

to lunch and standing in line for our food. Taking any other breaks during the workday was severely frowned upon.

22. The food was woefully inadequate. There was rice for breakfast, rice water soup for lunch, and rice and beans for dinner. On Sunday, we each received an egg and a cookie. Two or three times a week we had vegetables. Some very weak and elderly members received one egg per day. However, the food did improve markedly on the few occasions when there were outside visitors.

23. In contrast, Rev. Jones, claiming problems with his blood sugar, dined separately and ate meat regularly. He had his own refrigerator which was stocked with food. The two women with whom he resided, Maria Katsaris and Carolyn Layton, and the two small boys who lived with him, Kimo Prokes and John Stoen, dined with the membership. However, they were in much better physical shape than everyone else since they were also allowed to eat the food in Rev. Jones's refrigerator.

24. In February, 1978, conditions had become so bad that half of Jonestown was ill with severe diarrhea and high fevers. I was seriously ill for two weeks. Like most of the other sick people, I was not given any nourishing foods to help recover. I was given water and a tea drink until I was well enough to return to the basic rice and beans diet.

25. As the former financial secretary, I was

aware that the Temple received over $65,000 in
Social Security checks per month. It made me
angry to see that only a fraction of the income of
the senior citizens in the care of the Temple was
being used for their benefit. Some of the money
was being used to build a settlement that would
earn Rev. Jones the place in history with which
he was so obsessed. The balance was being held
in "reserve." Although I felt terrible about what
was happening, I was afraid to say anything because I knew that anyone with a differing opinion
gained the wrath of Jones and other members.

26. Rev. Jones's thoughts were made known to
the population of Jonestown by means of broadcasts over the loudspeaker system. He broadcast
an average of six hours per day. When the Reverend was particularly agitated, he would broadcast
for hours on end. He would talk on and on while
we worked in the fields or tried to sleep. In addi-
tion to the daily broadcasts, there were marathon
meetings six nights per week.

27. The tenor of the broadcasts revealed that
Rev. Jones's paranoia had reached an all-time
high. He was irate at the light in which he had
been protrayed by the media. He felt that as a
consequence of having been ridiculed and
maligned, he would be denied a place in history.
His obsession with his place in history was ma-
niacal. When pondering the loss of what he considered his rightful place in history, he would
grow despondent and say that all was lost.

28. Visitors were infrequently permitted access to Jonestown. The entire community was required to put on a performance when a visitor arrived. Before the visitor arrived, Rev. Jones would instruct us on the image we were to project. The workday would be shortened. The food would be better. Sometimes there would be music and dancing. Aside from these performances, there was little joy or hope in any of our lives. An air of despondency prevailed.

29. There was constant talk of death. In the early days of the People's Temple, general rhetoric about dying for principles was sometimes heard. In Jonestown, the concept of mass suicide for socialism arose. Because our lives were so wretched anyway and because we were so afraid to contradict Rev. Jones, the concept was not challenged.

30. An event which transpired shortly after I reached Jonestown convinced me that Rev. Jones had sufficient control over the minds of the residents that it would be possible for him to effect a mass suicide.

31. At least once a week, Rev. Jones would declare a "white night," or state of emergency. The entire population of Jonestown would be awakened by blaring sirens. Designated persons, approximately fifty in number, would arm themselves with rifles, move from cabin to cabin, and make certain that all members were responding. A mass meeting would ensue. Frequently during

these crises, we would be told that the jungle was swarming with mercenaries and that death could be expected at any minute.

32. During one "white night," we were informed that our situation had become hopeless and that the only course of action open to us was a mass suicide for the glory of socialism. We were told that we would be tortured by mercenaries if we were taken alive. Everyone, including the children, was told to line up. As we passed through the line, we were given a small glass of red liquid to drink. We were told that the liquid contained poison and that we would die within forty-five minutes. We all did as we were told. When the time came when we should have dropped dead, Rev. Jones explained that the poison was not real and that we had just been through a loyalty test. He warned us that the time was not far off when it would become necessary for us to die by our own hands.

33. Life at Jonestown was so miserable and the physical pain of exhaustion was so great that this event was not traumatic for me. I had become indifferent as to whether I lived or died.

34. During another "white night," I watched Carolyn Layton, my former sister-in-law, give sleeping pills to two young children in her care, John Victor Stoen and Kimo Prokes, her own son. Carolyn said to me that Rev. Jones had told her that everyone was going to have to die that night. She said that she would probably have to

shoot John and Kimo and that it would be easier for them if she did it while they were asleep.

35. In April, 1978, I was reassigned to Georgetown. I became determined to escape or die trying. I surreptitiously contacted my sister, who wired me a plane ticket. After I received the ticket, I sought the assistance of the United States Embassy in arranging to leave Guyana. Rev. Jones had instructed us that he had a spy working in the United States Embassy and that he would know if anyone went to the embassy for help. For this reason, I was very fearful.

36. I am most grateful to the United States government and Richard McCoy and Daniel Weber, in particular, for the assistance they gave me. However, the efforts made to investigate conditions in Jonestown are inadequate for the following reasons. The infrequent visits are always announced and arranged. Acting in fear for their lives, Temple members respond as they are told. The members appear to speak freely to American representatives, but in fact they are drilled thoroughly prior to each visit on what questions to expect and how to respond. Members are afraid of retaliation if they speak their true feelings in public.

37. On behalf of the population of Jonestown, I urge that the United States Government take adequate steps to safeguard their rights. I believe that their lives are in danger.

I declare under penalty of perjury that the

foregoing is true and correct, except as to those matters stated on information and belief and as to those I believe them to be true.

Executed this 15 day of June, 1978 at San Francisco, California.

Deborah Layton Blakey

Appendix 4
Temple Memorabilia

Here are samples of the "special offers," "miracle letters" and other propaganda provided by the People's Temple to entice unsuspecting and well-meaning men and women to support "the cause" of Jim Jones.

JIM V. JONES,
PASTOR
PEOPLES TEMPLE
P. O. BOX 214
REDWOOD VALLEY
CALIFORNIA 95470

Dear One,

Pastor Jim Jones has asked me to write to you to tell you that he cares very much for you and meditates often for your problems. He desires that your life be blessed and that your body be free from pain. In these past few weeks your needs and problems have been very much on his mind and he wants to help you RIGHT NOW in your time of need.

The ANOINTED PRAYER CLOTH in the small envelope enclosed has been blessed for you. To receive the greatest blessings from this Prayer Cloth follow these instructions:

1. Pin your Prayer Cloth to your clothing today.
2. Wear it for two days and two nights.
3. Send it in with your Prayer Sheet which is on the next page.

Pastor Jones will meditate for your needs using your Prayer Sheet and Prayer Cloth for seven days. You can help him by carefully filling in each part of the Prayer Sheet and sending it back quickly. If you would like Prayer Cloths to be sent to your loved ones and friends include their names and addresses with your letter, and they will be sent out immediately, as soon as they have been anointed.

Special blessings come to those who honor this work of God with their offerings. In recent meetings there has been a revelation about OBEDIENCE OFFERINGS of certain amounts. There are many who have been blessed when they gave as much as $700.00 or $999.00, and hundreds of others who received their miracles when they gave obediently as they were led by the Spirit. To know what your OBEDIENCE OFFERING should be, close your eyes and ask God to show you. When you ask with an honest heart you will be shown just how much you should give.

God will also reveal to Pastor Jones what your obedience offering should be. It is important that you be honest with God! Remember, "His affection is more abundant toward you, while he remembereth the obedience of you." (II Cor. 7.15) Through your faithful obedience blessings can begin to flow your way — as you have always hoped and dreamed that they would.

———— With many blessings,

Karen Layton,
Personal Secretary to Jim V. Jones

$328

Dorothy Hendrith

"I was in the service when the offering was being taken, and I emptied out my little billfold with all I had. It was only 20 cents and I didn't know where I would get any more money. But I thank God, when the mailman came I looked and there were two unexpected checks - $328.00 - to my surprise! I know it was you. I thank God and I thank you from the depths of my heart."

$177

"When my pastor said that $7.77 could cause financial blessings I gave that amount. The very next week I received a check in the mail that I did not expect or have any reason to receive for $177.00. I believe in miracles because I see them happening every day in my life."

Lucille Taylor

$800

Alberta Lindsay

"After I received your encouraging letter, Pastor Jones, a man who had owed us $700 repaid me. When I got home my husband and I counted out the $700 and I thought that was all. Then something made me look again into my purse. To my surprise there were five more $20 bills. I could hardly believe it! Thank God and thank you, Pastor Jones."

$13.77

"I gave $13.77, the amount that Pastor Jones has called the 'Miracle Obedience Offering.' That night on my way home I was glad I did. A stranger stepped up to my car at a stop sign. He had a long knife and tried to attack me through my open window, but I felt as if a 'protective shield' was around my car. The stranger couldn't get his knife close to my body, and he suddenly turned around and fled in terror."

Edith Bogue

$69

"I was in the service and gave $7.00 when Pastor Jones said this amount could bring special blessings. When I got my mail the next Monday morning I found an unexpected check there for $69.00. Shortly after that my last car payment was due, but before I could pay it, my pink slip came in the mail with a note from the bank thanking me for completing payment of my car."

Velma Darnes

$77

"I had money multiply in a beautiful meeting in Peoples Temple. During the offering when Pastor Jones asked if anyone had $7.00 I put this amount in. I looked again and $77.00 had miraculously materialized in my wallet. Praise God!"

Annie Moore

Personal
PRAYER SHEET
for: _____
Place your name here

Address _____

City _____ Zip Code _____

Telephone _____ Birthdate _____

HERE IS MY OBEDIENCE OFFERING _____

Pray for Me: _____
_____
_____
_____
_____

Here is the Prayer Cloth you sent to me. I have worn it for 2 days and 2 nights. Now I am asking you to meditate upon it as you pray for my needs.

Pray for My Healing Needs: _____
_____
_____
_____

Pray for My Financial Needs: _____
_____
_____
_____

Pray for My Spiritual Needs: _____
_____
_____
_____

Pray for My Loved Ones: _____
_____
_____
_____
_____

Report of My Visit to a Hungry or Lonely Person

Dear Pastor Jones,   Date_____

Today as you instructed I visited

_____
(name of person visited)

_____
(address of person visited)

_____   _____   _____
city   state   zip code

The food I took with me was_____

My personal message to the Pastor _____

_____

_____

_____

Here is my THANKSGIVING OFFERING. I am so grateful for my blessings! $_____

My Name_____ Phone Number _____

Address _____

City, State, Zip _____

It is important for you to fill out this sheet after you have made the visit requested by Pastor Jones.
Send the completed sheet to:
        Pastor Jim Jones, P.O. Box 214, Redwood Valley, California 95470.

Acknowledgments

To Marguerite Shuster and Paul Scotchmer for their research and writing skills.

To my secretaries, Glory Arnold, Dolores Loeding, Zera Wils, Joy Taylor, and Jeri Welbourne.

To Richard Baltzell, my editor at Fleming H. Revell Company.

To my wife, Lyla, and my children, Erin and Michael, who are always my best allies and critics.

DECEIVED is also a motion picture for use with the book in schools or churches.

The film tells the story of these defectors from the People's Temple and is available through your local religious film library or from Gospel Films, Inc., P.O. Box 455, Muskegon, Michigan 49443.